Easy-to-Manage

Reading & Writing
Conferences

Practical Ideas for Making Conferences Work

SCHOLASTIC
PROFESSIONAL BOOKS

NEW YORK • TORONTO • LONDON • AUCKLAND • SYDNEY

With love for the Indiana Robbs,

Steve, Maggie, and Douglas.

— L. R.

Cover and interior design by Kathy Massaro
Cover photo and interior photos by Bonnie Forstrum Jacobs

ISBN: 0-590-31441-6
Copyright © 1998 by Laura Robb
All rights reserved.
Printed in the U.S.A.

Contents

Introduction

Several years ago I spent two unforgettable days in teacher Angie Littleton's fourth-grade classroom. Angie had asked me to observe her reading and writing conferences, explaining prior to my visit, "I need to adjust the amount of time I spend on conferences." She looked to me to help her make conferences work—and she sounded overwhelmed.

Indeed, by the close of my first day in her classroom, Angie was exhausted. On the second day, after Angie had dismissed her twenty-two students, she rescheduled our after-school meeting. "I have to use the time to write up worksheets for tomorrow. If I don't, I won't be able to hold conferences. While I confer with one group, the other two groups can be busy filling in their sheets," she explained.

A dedicated and extraordinarily hardworking teacher, Angie tried to hold a 20-minute reading or writing conference with each student once every two weeks. To gain more time, she worked long hours preparing individual and group worksheets that would enable her students to work independently while she held conferences.

Angie's day was so tightly scheduled with conferences that she became impatient with students who couldn't figure out the directions on the worksheets. A hurried tone dominated the class. By devoting a large chunk of her time to conferences, Angie had little time for direct teaching and reflection. Frazzled, Angie confessed, "I can't even squeeze in mini-lessons. I'm beginning to hate these conferences."

During our conversations, I discovered that Angie equated being an outstanding teacher with her ability to see each student for 20 minutes twice a month and to confer daily with various groups.

I could relate. Several years ago I had tried to schedule, every two weeks, 25-minute reading-writing conferences with each of 24 students. It's a hoop we were all trying to jump through, as it seemed one of the golden rules of writing and reading workshops. The first week I introduced such conferences was always terrific, but as soon as I had to weave in school-mandated schedule changes or meet with groups of students who needed additional help, the schedule deteriorated. By the end of the first month I was so behind, I knew I would never catch up.

Unfortunately, too many teachers feel pressured to conduct ongoing, lengthy one-on-one conferences. As Angie lamented, "That's what terrific teachers do." In a short time, many, like Angie, hate the process and flirt with giving it up altogether.

Yet conferring supports young readers and writers greatly. It's at the heart of good teaching, and Angie understood this. The issue for her was not whether to abandon the practice but how to make it practical. She needed to find a way to integrate conferences into a classroom schedule so that students' needs would be quickly addressed without overwhelming her. "How did you make it work?" she asked me, and I shared what I had learned.

First, I redefined my idea of a conference, moving away from the standard of the 20-minute conference, and experimented with short meetings that focused on a single issue. I turned over to my students some of the responsibility for conferring. This reduced my stress and revealed to me the power of peers helping one another. I explored the art of conferring, refining my ability to ask questions that would quickly lead to the heart of a student's concern. I learned to listen carefully, and with greater openness. And as I got better at conferring, my students did too, and together we discovered a variety of easy-to-manage conferences. The word *confer* comes from the Latin word *conferre*, meaning "to bring together" (from *com*, "together,"+ *ferre,* "to carry"), and that's the effect this practice had on us. It brought my students and me together, and collectively, we carried the weight of conferences on many shoulders.

An important goal of this book is to lighten your load by providing you with a menu of conferences that can easily fit into the school day. I've included management and scheduling tips as well as record-keeping forms that won't overwhelm you.

Acknowledgments

The poet John Donne's famous words, "No man is an island, entire of itself; every man is a piece of the continent," remind me how my life—including the life of this book—is linked to family, friends, students, and colleagues. The impetus to write this book springs from relationships with many people within and outside of education, whose suggestions, research, and experiences I wove into the text.

Thanks to the students whose work appears in this book. Their feedback enabled me to refine conference forms and records so that they were easy to follow and easy to manage.

Thanks to Ellen Benjamin and Mary Barnes—fourth- and fifth-grade teachers at Powhatan School in Boyce, Virginia, where I teach—who invited me into their classrooms to confer with their students. I owe a special gratitude to John Lathrop, head of Powhatan, whose support enabled me to research and write throughout the school year.

Thanks to Heather Campbell, fourth-grade teacher at Quarles Elementary in Winchester, Virginia, and Sandy Palmer, fourth-grade teacher at W. H. Keister Elementary School in Harrisonburg, Virginia, both of whom were willing to explore new terrain and contribute wonderful student work and adaptations of suggestions. Thanks as well to the principal of Quarles, Nancy Lee, and the principal of W. H. Keister, Ann Conners, who nurture their teachers and encourage them to take risks by implementing research-based innovative teaching practices.

I also want to express my appreciation to Terry Cooper, Editor in Chief of Scholastic Professional Books, who suggested the idea for this book, and to Wendy Murray, a nurturing and sensitive editor, who read drafts, made excellent suggestions, and helped me shape the book into its final form.

And to my husband, Lloyd, my deepest thanks and appreciation. Throughout the writing of the book, he listened to me talk about problems, discussed students' responses, and studied students' samples. He brought fresh eyes and positive suggestions to drafts of each chapter, and our conversations about teaching and learning have had a profound influence on my thinking about conferences, reading, and writing.

CHAPTER 1

The Benefits and Basics of Implementing Conferences

I didn't exactly plan to reenvision the way I approached conferences. Like many of my teaching discoveries, the revamp occurred after I hit a brick wall.

I'd given my fifth graders a series of writing mini-lessons on the show-don't-tell technique, demonstrating how good writers *show* what the sunset looks like rather than stating "The sky is pretty." For six lessons over the course of two weeks, I modeled this writing tool with my own prose and with passages from favorite writers such as Jean Van Leeuwen (*Bound for Oregon*) and Katherine Paterson (*Flip-Flop Girl*).

After each mini-lesson, students used the remainder of the writing workshop to draft memoirs that focused on a single childhood experience. They were to work with dialogue, specific details, thoughts, and figurative language to describe their experiences.

On the due date, I collected their pieces. That evening, comfortably curled up on an overstuffed wing chair, I read my students' drafts. Two hours later, I'd completed half the papers and discovered that only four kids understood the mini-lessons, three had made a good start, and five wrote sentences like "I was scared. My brother is mean. Mom was sleepy." No details. No descriptions. No dialogue. I was so discouraged; I had worked so carefully preparing demonstrations. Sitting in my armchair, I knew I had to try something new. It was clear that everyone doesn't "get it" through mini-lessons alone, even if they are sustained over a period of time, and writing detailed comments in the margins of their papers wasn't going to do the trick either. How could I reach and teach those kids who weren't getting it, before they struggled and handed in work that missed the mark? The answer, I discovered, was five- to ten-minute conferences following the mini-lessons. Children's writing improved significantly once I'd instituted these brief "spot checks" that provided immediate feedback to questions. This was the first step toward integrating a variety of conferences into my teaching.

Conferences: Opportunities to Problem-Solve

"I got it after we worked together." "Now I see it." "When you're close to me, I understand more." These are typical comments from students who briefly worked with me to clarify the content of a reading or writing mini-lesson.

Quite often, children who are not connecting to a demonstration hear and observe little. Kids tell me that if a demonstration confuses them, they stop listening and observing. Sometimes their minds are bombarded by worried thoughts like "This is too hard. I don't get it." During a one-on-one exchange, students have the opportunity to hear, once more, the

The Mini-Lesson Defined

Developed by Nancie Atwell and Lucy Calkins, the mini-lesson is a brief, focused session—usually about 10 minutes—that teaches writing or reading strategies through demonstration. The purpose of these information-packed monologues is to allow learners to observe how a peer or the teacher uses a strategy. Lively discussion follows mini-lessons, as students exchange ideas, raise questions, and share how they apply the strategy to their work.

highlights of the mini-lesson, to ask questions they might be reluctant to pose in front of peers, and to practice the strategy before going off on their own. These short encounters can pinpoint those students who might benefit from several conferences.

Over time and through my experiences with a variety of conferences, I gained insights into students' learning styles and figured out ways to support them. Equally important, I soon recognized that the goal of all conferring was to offer students experiences that enabled them to confer with peers and with their own inner voices.

One-on-One Conferences: Nurturing Every Child

One-on-one meetings are the ultimate confidence-builders for students. They're especially effective as follow-ups to mini-lessons, when students practice a strategy. Your undivided attention to each child makes them feel that you care about their learning and will try to help them understand and improve.

As I circulate around the classroom, I visit with students who don't participate in post-mini-lesson discussions and those who have a difficult time settling into writing or reading. I try to visit eight to ten students a day and read the writing drafts and journal responses of four to five students.

At first you may be initiating the lion's share of the conferences and focusing on the kids who have tuned out. But in time, many students will request these one-on-one meetings.

Conferring With Groups: Letting Kids in on How Others Do It

Whole-class, small-group, and partner conferences provide opportunities for students to help one another. Students exchange all sorts of strategies, such as how they use dialogue in stories, organize notes before they write an essay, or figure out the pronunciation of a word. Often, seeing how a peer uses a writing or reading strategy offers just the method another child needs. When Sally told her fellow fourth graders, "Whenever I predict, I ask myself, 'What could happen next?' If I think 'could,' then I don't have to be right." Sighs of relief wafted through the room. Sally had provided students who thought their predictions had to be right with a new way of thinking about the strategy.

Teaching the How-To's of Conferences

Effective conferring is an acquired skill. You can teach your students how to participate by conducting conferences in front of the class. Much like a mini-lesson, these demos allow children to observe the process and then discuss what they saw.

Early in the school year I tell students that I will conduct a few kinds of conferences in front of the classroom so they can see how one-on-one and small-group conferences work. I call these center-stage conferences. I repeat them often, and students love them. They clamor to have a turn in the spotlight.

A Sample Center-Stage Writing Conference

Fifth-grader Jenny and I sit side by side in front of the class. I tell students the purpose of this one-on-one conference: Jenny's goal is to add dialogue to "Lost and Found," a story about the day she lost Sylvia, her springer spaniel puppy.

Robb: *Your story made me laugh when Sylvia slid out of your soapy hands as you bathed her in the yard.*

Quick Notes Offer Lasting Benefits

Most days when I make the rounds, I don't keep written records. It's too difficult and distracting—neither the student nor I can read and process a constant barrage of notes. Sometimes I'll jot an important point or suggestion on a dated sticky note that the child places in a journal or writing folder. For example, if a child's draft has few details, I'll ask her to generate questions about the topic. My sticky note will include one or two sample questions to get her started.

Jen: (giggles) You should have been there.

Robb: Your details put me there. You also made me feel sad when Sylvia ran away and you couldn't see her. I agree with your goal of adding dialogue. I think the conversation will help readers know how you feel. Read your piece out loud and put a check next to the places you could add dialogue.

[Jen reads and checks two places.]

Robb: I think questioning your neighbor and friend are two great places for dialogue. Do you think you might also include some of your inner thoughts? That way we know how you feel by what you think.

Jen: You mean like what Robert did in his story about getting lost.

Robb: Exactly.

Jen: I can look for places and then show you before I add.

Robb: You can also ask Robert for his suggestions and help.

Jen: I'll think about that.

Follow-Up Discussion: Pinpointing the Benefits

After Jen and I end the conference, I invite the other 24 fifth graders to pair up and talk for two to three minutes about all the positive things they noticed and jot down any questions they had. Here is what these fifth graders came up with:

❋ You started with nice things about the story.

❋ You said how it made you feel.

❋ Jenny looked at you. She listened.

❋ Jenny had her topic before the conference.

❋ Jenny said she'd think about getting Robert's help. She could decide.

Children seize this opportunity to sort out the intricacies of conferences. Riva and Kiwan revealed their sensitivity to the process with these questions:

Kiwan: Do students always have to have a question about their writing for a conference?

Robb: No. Often I or a partner will raise a question.

Riva: What if Jen couldn't find any places [for dialogue]?

Robb: I would show her one place and explain why I thought dialogue would work here. Then I'd ask Jen to try to find a place.

A Sample Center-Stage Reading Conference

Four seventh graders and I sit in a semicircle in front of the class. Our purpose is to share strategies they use for book selection. I chose these students because they, unlike most of their classmates, wrote on their reading surveys (see page 51) that they *loved* to read and even read at home. I wanted other students to learn from them. I start the conference by inviting students to explain how they choose books from the library.

Mara: I usually look for mysteries. I love suspense and being scared.

Jeff: I read mostly nonfiction about rockets and airplanes. I want to be an astronaut. I read to learn more about that.

Kyle: I'm not a fast reader, so I look for books that are easy to read. Sometimes I reread a book I liked a lot, like <u>What Jamie Saw</u> [by Carolyn Coman].

Rosa: I read horse books. I'm into the Black Stallion books. I wish I could have my own horse.

Robb: Sounds like you're reading books because you're really interested in a topic or a type of book. [Students nod] But how do you know if a book will be too hard or too easy?

The students take turns answering this last question. Kyle explains that she knows she can read the Black Stallion books, so there's no problem. Mara and Jeff start reading the first page. "If I can read most of the words and understand," said Mara, "then I figure I can read the book." Rosa, who struggles with reading, explained the five-finger method that she learned from special reading classes in fifth grade. "I open a page and read. If there are five words I can't say or don't understand, I try another book."

Afterward, their classmates share what they noticed:

☀ They read books on things that interested them.

☀ It's okay to read a book that's easy.

☀ I never thought of rereading a book.

☀ They all had ways to see if they could read and understand.

☀ They liked reading.

This class did not raise questions, and I did not press them. Instead, I took the opportunity to write on chart paper the strategies that students had offered for book selection. During the next two or three classes,

we would practice and discuss these strategies.

I hope these sample center-stage conferences have shown that you can discover conference topics in all sorts of ways. As you saw with the four seventh graders, conferences spring from students' difficulties and from their strengths, from their negative attitudes toward reading or writing and from their love of these subjects.

Key Teaching Guidelines for Reading and Writing Conferences

Before getting into the particulars of the various conferences, I'd like to share some general tips that will help them run smoothly in your classroom.

● KEEP A NURTURING TONE: Resist the temptation to dive into a correcting mode. Instead, open a conference by mentioning how the child's work affects you or by stating some terrific work habits you've observed. Even if you're casually making the rounds, start the conversation with relaxing words that let students know you're tuned into their reading and writing lives. The phrases that follow are some icebreakers that I've used:

"I see that you're writing another piece about that camping trip. I'll never forget how frightened I was reading about the rattlesnake. Is this piece going to be scary?"

"What detailed support you have for both predictions! How will you go about making adjustments?"

"I noticed that you're really into writing science fiction. What's this piece about?"

"Looks like you're thinking about what to write. How's it going?"

"I noticed you chuckling as you read your book. Do you want to share a humorous part with me or your classmates?"

"Your journal response shows two key decisions the main character made. How will you figure out ways these decisions changed her?"

- **GIVE STUDENTS TIME TO THINK:** Watch and listen carefully while you're making the rounds, and you'll pick up on the type of support a child needs. Then raise helpful questions such as "Would you like to talk about your idea?" or "I noticed that you're trying to paragraph your story. Can I help?" or "You haven't taken out your book yet? How can I help?"

  While the pause that follows such questions can seem like a year and a half, I've learned to wait it out. Don't give in to the impulse to fill the silence with suggestions. When kids have time to think through a reading or writing issue, their responses are much more thoughtful. A key goal of conferring is to allow students to develop their own problem-solving skills and instincts about their work. Give them time to collect their thoughts, and help them develop their inner voice.

- **FOLLOW UP WITH MORE QUESTIONS, NOT ANSWERS:** After a student answers your initial question, continue conferring by asking more questions. Resist the urge to find quick solutions for a student. Sometimes general questions such as "What makes you say that?" stimulate students to talk more openly.

- **LISTEN CAREFULLY FOR DISTRESS SIGNALS:** In the rush of classroom life, it's all too easy to brush past important signals students send you about difficulties they're having. For example, when a seventh grader told me, "I hate to read because I don't remember anything," I could have responded with a stock recommendation like "Try to read more slowly" and never have gotten to the bottom of his reading trouble. Instead I followed with, "Can you tell me why you have trouble remembering?"

  After a long pause, he replied, "Because I can say the words, but I don't know what most of them mean." His reply opened the door for a discussion of the frustration he felt and allowed me to diagnose that his reading difficulty was primarily due to a lack of a strong vocabulary.

  I asked the student to think of ways his teachers and parents could help him and to let me know at the next conference. I said I'd bring some suggestions, too. When we met, the seventh grader said, "I think it would help if I could get someone to help me read for science and history. And if you could help me find books I can read."

  I added a suggestion—that he work on enlarging his vocabulary—and gave him some strategies to try. We agreed to schedule five-minute check-ups every couple of weeks to evaluate his progress. The student also knew that he could request additional meetings with me.

- **SET GOALS:** During a conference, involve the student as much as possible in exploring options that support development in reading and writing. Incorporating a student's suggestions in a progress plan honors the child and motivates him or her to make an effort. The bonus is that students often have top-notch ideas!

Conference Guidelines for Students

- ❉ Come with materials.
- ❉ Make eye contact.
- ❉ Take the time to think.
- ❉ Ask questions when you don't understand.

- ❉ Help set reachable goals.
- ❉ Call for follow-up meetings if you feel you need them.

Guidelines for Teachers

- ❉ Create a relaxed atmosphere.
- ❉ Prevent interruptions from other students. This is a student's special time with you.
- ❉ Make eye contact.
- ❉ Be positive; help students identify their strengths and progress.
- ❉ Listen carefully.
- ❉ Let participants do most of the talking.
- ❉ Ask questions that help participants think about difficulties they're having.

- ❉ Take notes during the conference.
- ❉ Encourage participants to discover strategies for themselves.
- ❉ Offer choices when setting goals.
- ❉ Close with an upbeat comment, and make students aware of your support.
- ❉ Make a copy of the conference notes for your files. Have the student place the original in his or her reading log folder.

Key Management Ideas Behind Reading and Writing Conferences

- DEFINE CONFERENCE ROLES: Students learn to participate effectively in conferences through start-of-school center-stage conferences, regular classroom discussions, and experiences with conferences.

  Before you launch a center-stage demonstration, collaborate with students to develop guidelines for the leader and participants. It's helpful to record all ideas on large sheets of chart paper that you can then display for students to review and revise.

  My students in grades four and eight contributed to the suggestions in the box shown above.

- KEEP SIMPLE RECORDS: Years ago, I diligently developed different forms for each type of reading and writing conference.

Soon I had a form for revising, editing, journal-writing, reading strategy, and reading-fluency conferences, to name just a few! Forms filled students' folders and piled up on my desk, waiting to be filed. Often I'd bring the wrong form to a conference and end up taking notes on lined paper. Once I recognized that forms were ruling me, I developed a form that can be used for a reading or writing conference on any topic.

I like to fill out the form during conferences and give it to students to store in their writing folders or response journals, which remain at school. This way, the notes are always handy for kids to refer to and they're available to me to review or share with colleagues, parents, or administrators.

Conference Form for Students

Name _____ **Date** _____

____ Reading Conference   ____ Writing Conference

☀ Topic:

☀ List what was discussed. (Start with the positives, then list needs).

☀ How do you plan to use what you have learned?

☀ Do you need to schedule another conference?

☀ List suggested times for another conference.

CONFERENCE FORM FOR STUDENTS

Name Jimmy _____ Date 11/4/96

✓ Reading Conference ___ Writing Conference

Topic: October reading contract

List What Was Discussed
· Jimmy's reading contract for October— he committed to 2 books and has not completed his contract.
· Showed J. his contract and log and asked him to explain what happened: 2nd book not done.
· One book was read—not entered.

How Do You Plan To Use What You Have Learned?
· Jimmy explained that he kept putting off finding and reading a second book. He worried about meeting his Nov. contract and making up this work. Together we negotiated that Jimmy would read a book over Thanksgiving break.

Do You Need To Schedule Another Conference? Yes— we met during lunch and together her selected 3 titles Jimmy could choose from and read over his holiday.

List Suggested Times For Another Conference
1st week in December—

CONFERENCE FORM FOR STUDENTS

Name Sally S. _____ Date 2/27/97

___ Reading Conference ✓ Writing Conference

Topic: Questions Sally raised about the chapter book she's writing.

List What Was Discussed
· Is the scene where Kendall acts upset when her best friend is killed in a hit and run accident realistic and emotionally powerful enough?
· In the story Sally had Kendall run to her room after witnessing the accident, then fall asleep. When Kendall awoke, she thought the accident was a dream.
· I asked Sally to think about how she would react and feel

How Do You Plan To Use What You Have Learned? and do.
· Changes Sally will work on—based on her thoughts:
· Maybe K. is alive—run to the body—try to wake her.
· I'd be scared once I realized she was dead.
· I'd scream for help—then run to my room—sob and deal with my thoughts—blame myself, anger, fears

Do You Need To Schedule Another Conference? No—just let me read your rewrite—then we can decide if we need to confer again.

List Suggested Times For Another Conference

An eighth grader's reading conference addresses incomplete work (top). *A writing conference form is a useful tool to help guide revision* (above).

● HOLD CONFERENCES IN A SPECIAL PLACE: Most conferences will occur in the classroom as you move from student to student or join a group at their regular seats. That said, it's important to create a special place for longer conferences. You might place a small table or desk in the corner of your room, perhaps with a sign that reads "Conference Corner" to create a sense of intimacy. If your classroom is small, you can hold conferences in the hall.

● OFFER "RIGHT-NOW" AND "TEN MINUTES" SIGN-UPS: On the chalkboard in my classroom are two headings: "Right Now" and "Ten Minutes." Students with burning needs can sign up for "Right Now"—which stands for *please see me as soon as possible*—or "Ten Minutes," if they need a longer but not pressing meeting. Giving children these two options encourages them to reflect on their needs prior to signing up for extra help.

Students sign up throughout workshop, though as the year goes on, many solve their problems with peer help. If the list is unusually long, it might take two days for me to see every child.

● SEEK OUT STUDENT HELPERS: While making the rounds, note the names of possible peer helpers on sticky notes. Since I can't possibly attend to the needs of 24 students, it's crucial that I teach students how to support one another and themselves. Posted on chart paper are the guidelines students follow when I'm meeting with a group or one student:

Guidelines for Extra Help

1. Try to help yourself. Look at the sticky notes from past conferences that are in your folder. Reread the chart(s) on that topic.

2. Seek help from a classmate who is an "expert" on the topic.

3. Put your name on the chalkboard under "Right Now" or "Ten Minutes."

4. If you can't move forward, work on another project until you receive help.

Key Assessment Principles Behind Reading and Writing Conferences

- BASE TOPICS FOR CONFERENCES ON STUDENTS' NEEDS: Throughout this book you'll glean ideas for conference topics, but you won't find a ready-made list or a magic sequence of topics; these have to arise from your own classroom.

  Conferences are meaningful and productive only when they reflect your students' prior knowledge, skill level, and the tone of your teaching.

  You'll find that what students say and do in reading and writing will provide you with more to discuss than there is time to address.

- ENCOURAGE STUDENTS' SELF-REFLECTION: Fostering students' ability to think about their work in reading and writing helps them recognize matters they need assistance with—matters that often make meaningful conference topics. Here are some ways to promote self-reflection:

  - ☀ While making the rounds, invite students to pause and think about reading and writing. Let them tell you what kind of support they require.

  - ☀ Teach students to reread their writing to evaluate leads, endings, details, and punctuation. Then provide them with suggestions to improve these things.

  - ☀ Have students check their writing against established guidelines. Ask them to think about guidelines that need to be added and/or improved.

  - ☀ Encourage students to identify words, phrases, and passages they don't comprehend. Provide them with strategies that foster comprehension, such as rereading and using context clues to figure out words that stump them.

  - ☀ During mini-lessons and throughout the day, think aloud and show students how you come up with reading and writing topics. Show them how you figure out what strategies to try.

- TAP INTO WHAT PARENTS KNOW ABOUT THEIR CHILD: Adapt the Parent Information Sheet (see next page) to send home at the start of school. Parents' responses will give you information that will help you teach and confer with the child all year long.

  Rarely do I have to call to remind a parent to fill out an Information Sheet and return it to school.

△△△△△△△△△△△△△△△ TIP BOX △△△△△△△△△△△△△△△

Make the Most of Mini-lessons

Write all your mini-lessons on chart paper, date them, and display them on the walls for students to consult. Over time, store mini-lesson charts in a closet by clipping them to skirt hangers. Post a running list of mini-lessons that includes date and subject so that students can easily access stored charts.

Parent Information Sheet

Child's Name _____ **Date** _____

Teacher _____

Please answer the questions that follow. The information you give can help me help your child learn. I value what you know about your child and look forward to working together this year to meet your child's needs.

* Please list all of your child's strong points.

* What are your child's interests and hobbies?

* What do you and your child enjoy doing together?

* Any tips or suggestions that might help your child learn?

* When is the best time to call you?

Here are some sample parent responses that Heather Campbell, a fourth-grade teacher, and I received from parents:

Please list all your child's strong points:

PARENTS' COMMENTS: GRADE 4

☀ Crystal is outgoing and happy-go-lucky and very flexible.

☀ Cries easily. Has a temper and often doesn't listen.

☀ Noel is very determined to succeed in what she starts. Loves to read.

☀ Outstanding athlete. Makes friends easily. Loves the outdoors.

PARENTS' COMMENTS: GRADE 8

☀ He's a peacemaker and a self-starter.

☀ Sara is outgoing and wants to do well in school. She is very strong-willed and social.

☀ Diligent, meticulous—never gives up.

Any tips or suggestions that might help your child learn?

PARENTS' COMMENTS: GRADE 8

☀ Explain directions fully. Anne is a visual learner.

☀ Hunter does not deal well with frustration, which creates a difficult balance between challenging and overwhelming him.

☀ He needs help in getting organized.

☀ If Wesley can be stroked and recognized for progress, it makes a tremendous difference.

Sending home Information Sheets at the start of the school year provides you with a wealth of insights about students.

PARENTS' COMMENTS: GRADE 4

☀ Stephanie is very shy and doesn't like to be put on the spot.

☀ Make sure she understands classroom instructions.

☀ Needs quiet when reading— no distractions.

INFORMATION SHEET

Child's Name _Beth Morgan_ Date _9-10-96_
Teacher _Mrs. Foreman_

Please answer the questions that follow. The information you give can help me help your child learn. I value what you know about your child and look forward to working together this year to meet your child's needs.

Please list all of your child's strong points.
Sensitive to other peoples needs.
Follows thru on task does not need to be reminded very often.
Takes ~~initiative~~ initiative to help others.

What are your child's interests and hobbies?
dogs   outdoor activities
monkey's   Insect collecting
Reading   Creative play; dress-up
Crafts

What do you and your child enjoy doing together?
Fishing   Walking
Camping   hiking
Crafts

Any tips or suggestions that might help your child learn?
Make sure she understands Classroom instructions.

INFORMATION SHEET

Child's Name _MATT FAUNING_ Date _9/9/96_
Teacher _MRS. LAURA ROBB_

Please answer the questions that follow. The information you give can help me help your child learn. I value what you know about your child and look forward to working together this year to meet your child's needs.

Please list all of your child's strong points.
① SENSITIVE
② VERY IN TOUCH WITH HIMSELF   ⑧ SINCERE FRIEND
③ STRONG SENSE OF RIGHT & WRONG ⑨ CONSCIENTIOUS
④ FAIR MINDED
⑤ GOOD SENSE OF HUMOR
⑥ SPIRITUAL
⑦ LOVES CHILDREN

What are your child's interests and hobbies?
① BASKETBALL (GREATEST LOVE)   ⑦ CHURCH YOUTH ACTIVITIES
② SOCCER
③ SWIMMING
④ MUSIC
⑤ VIDEO GAMES
⑥ COLLECTING SPORT CARDS

What do you and your child enjoy doing together?
① TALKING & SHARING FEELINGS
② LISTENING TO MUSIC
③ WATCHING SPORTS
④ PARTICIPATING IN SPORTS

Any tips or suggestions that might help your child learn?
① NEEDS TO GAIN A BETTER APPRECIATION FOR READING
② NEEDS DETAILED INSTRUCTION
③ NEEDS POSITIVE REINFORCEMENT AS OPPOSED TO WHAT MIGHT BE INTERPRETED AS CRITISISM.

When is the best time to call you?
I WORK M-W-F 8:30-12:30. I'LL ON THE GO ALOT, BUT DO HAVE A MACHINE IF YOU CAN'T REACH ME. EARLY TUES. OR THURS. MAY BE BEST OR AFTER 8:00 PM.

Three-Way Conferences: Parent, Teacher, and Student

Parents value conferences led by their child. These meetings open meaningful communication as children explain what they have learned, how they have progressed, and discuss their goals. Together, the child and I field parent's questions.

By reviewing written work and having opportunities to question their child and the teacher, parents look at concrete evidence of what their child is learning. Moreover, the fact that the child leads the conference illustrates the depth of a student's awareness as he articulates growth, progress, and future goals. Parents make comments such as, "Joey helped me understand how he is working on spelling,

Three Ways to Find Topics

The following strategies will enable you to establish timely and meaningful conference topics based on students' needs:

 Observe students at work. When students read and write independently, watch what they do—and don't do. For example, during a seventh-grade writing workshop, I watched a girl crumple up and toss a piece a paper into the trash can and then start writing on a new sheet of paper. After she did this with five sheets of paper, I approached her. "I can't get started," she told me, her voice laced with frustration. I spent five minutes with her, peppering her with questions to get her ideas flowing. Soon she was excitedly describing her first camping experience. Halfway through her telling, she switched from talking to brainstorming on paper.

 Listen to students talk. When students work in pairs or small groups, circulate and listen. During a group book-discussion, a sixth grader told his classmates, "I can't find an example. I don't know what this book's about." The next day, while making the rounds, I repeated the remark and asked the child, "How can I support you?" After a pause that felt like an eternity, the reply came: "Find me a book where I can read the words."

 Scan students' journal entries and other writing. When reading students' writing, it's important to focus on what's working, but sometimes it's necessary to provide students with helpful strategies during first drafts. Greg, a seventh grader, started his stories with a capital letter and two pages later placed a period. Sixth-grader Ginger made excellent predictions in her reading journal but rarely gave supporting examples from the story. Quick conferences with me and peers helped both students move forward.

and I even say improvement," or "When I read the pages from Maria's literature response journal, I began to understand how she was thinking about the books she's reading." Such remarks illustrate that the specific examples students share can enlist the support of parents for teaching practices that differ from families' personal experiences.

In addition to the scheduled conferences at school, several times during the year, students write letters home about a project, a book, a piece of writing or research, and invite parents to react by writing back. Often students ask parents to write about their school days.

Powhatan School
Rt. 1, Box 177A
Boyce, VA 22620
December 11, 1996

Dear Mom,

I am having a blast in English class with Mrs. Robb this year. I am learning so much.
In writing I am learning how to revise papers that I have written, also I learned that the best thing a writer can do is to read out loud what you have just written so it is easier to catch your mistakes.
Grammar is going very well. Now, we are studying verbs and prepositions. Mrs. Robb makes grammar much easier because we apply everything to all the free choice pieces poems, and essays we write.
We do a lot of writing in her class. We usually write about a book that we have read. There sure is plenty of work to do in English, but most of it is not very difficult. We get lots of homework, but I guess it is reasonable.

Our English class is always moving. That is what I like about Mrs. Robb, her class is never boring. We have group discussions on books that we read in class.
Mom, could you please write back to me about what you think, also, please tell me a little about your eighth grade English class.

Love,
Tyler

P.S.
You are going to be invited to come visit our English class for a presentation.

An eighth grader writes to his mother and explains what he's learning.

263 Bowling Green Road
Front Royal, Virginia 22630
Noember 18, 1996

Dear Tyler,

Thank you for the nice letter you sent me about what you have learned in Mrs. Robb's English class. I have made several observations concerning your progress .

Your writing skills have improved greatly since last spring. I notice every word is spelled correctly, your puncuation is correct and your sentences are formed with care. The most delightful change I see is how well your thoughts are organized , helping your prose to flow. Having taught grammar and writing a very long time ago, I certainly can see that you are taking great care to make your writing "readable".

It pleases me that not only are you reading more stories, but enjoying what you are reading. I know in the past you have considered reading to be a chore, but I can see a change in that pattern also. The books and short stories you and Mrs. Robb are choosing are ones that excite you . Excitement about reading happens throughout your life, and I hope you will continue down this path.

My writing skills in eighth grade were not as refined as yours. We did not learn editing, which I consider to be a fine art. In my English class, we spent too much time reading passages from workbooks and answering questions about what we had read. I never enjoyed that part of class, but I always looked forward to reading novels and participating in class discussions. We read The Scarlet Letter and Silas Marner when I was in eighth grade, (it must surprise you that I remember that!). Characters in books would become friends of mine that I always remember, even now.

My favorite English activity always centered around learning new words and spelling them correctly. I loved the spelling bees, trying to spell words I had never heard before. I think in eighth grade I began to see newly-learned words "jump" out at me in other places right after I had seen them. Have you ever had that happen to you?

Thank you again for writing to me. Continue progressing as well as you have and I am sure your English teachers in ninth grade will be most appreciative.

Love,

Mom

The parent writes back to her child.

This process keeps parents abreast of what's happening in the classroom and honors their experiences. The letters can also serve to open a conversation about school during a parent-student-teacher conference.

A Menu of Easy-to-Manage Conferences

I n this section you'll explore a variety of conferences. The purpose of this overview is to show you that you have choices. Select those conferences that best serve you and your students' learning. Don't try to integrate all these conferences at once; select one type and add another when you and students have worked out the kinks and are comfortable with the process. In the chart that follows, under "Just Beginning" are conferences that are ideal if you've just begun to introduce conferences into your classroom.

Conference Menu

JUST BEGINNING

Teacher Observation Conference
(See pages 24–28.)

Organization: whole class and/or groups working independently

Purpose: to observe what students do well

Time: 15 to 30 minutes

Making the Rounds Conference
(See pages 37– 41.)

Organization: whole class

Purpose: to frequently confer with students to determine their progress and special needs

Time: 2 minutes with each student

Spotlighting Conference
(See pages 28–30.)

Organization: whole class and/or groups working independently as the teacher circulates to observe students' work

Purpose: to "spotlight" one or two students who "get it" and discuss their process with the class

Time: 5 to 10 minutes

Debriefing Conference
(See pages 30–32.)

Organization: whole class, small groups, or pairs evaluate a strategy, skill, or technique

Purpose: to highlight what worked, identify areas that could improve, and offer suggestions for change

Time: 10 to 15 minutes

Focus Conference   *(See pages 41–43.)*

Organization: one student or a small group confers with the teacher

Purpose: to concentrate on one issue in reading or writing, to directly intervene and support students, or to confer about a book

Time: 5 to 10 minutes

Parent-Teacher Conference
(See pages 131–133.)

Organization: parents and teacher (sometimes the child is brought into the conference after the adults have conferred)

Purpose: to evaluate a child's strengths and needs, to set learning goals, to keep parents abreast of classroom practices, and to enlist home support

Time: 15 to 20 minutes

Traditional Teacher-Led Student Conference
(See pages 81–84.)

Organization: two to six students and the teacher

Purpose: to collect data about a student or to support a struggling student

Time: 20 to 25 minutes

Teacher-Led Small-Group Conference
(See pages 33–34.)

Organization: two to six students and the teacher

Purpose: to monitor book discussions or to support students who have common problems

Time: 10 to 20 minutes

Teacher-Led Group-Share Writing Conference
(See pages 109–110.)

Organization: whole class or small group

Purpose: to model how to give positive feedback to student writers or to provide a forum for peer and teacher support

Time: 10 to 20 minutes

Teacher-Led Book Conference
(See pages 88–90.)

Organization: teacher and one student

Purpose: to engage students in reflection about a completed book

Time: 10 to 12 minutes

Student-Led Partner or Group Conference
(See pages 34–36.)

Organization: two to six students

Purpose: to allow students to confer about books, writing, and research

Time: 5 to 20 minutes

Solo Conference
(See pages 43–44.)

Organization: student confers with self

Purpose: to encourage students to solve reading and writing problems on their own and to encourage self-evaluation

Time: 5 to 15 minutes

Student-Led Parent Conference
(See pages 133–140.)

Organization: students and families confer about students' work at home or at school

Purpose: to enable students to discuss their work and progress with families, to have adults write to students to celebrate their growth, and to encourage parents to set reasonable goals with their children

Time: 15 to 25 minutes

Student-Led Parent-Teacher Conference
(See pages 141–142.)

Organization: student, teacher, and family members

Purpose: to enable students to discuss their work, progress, and goals in a three-way conference and to have adults respond to the conference in writing

Time: 20 to 25 minutes

General Guidelines

As you think about the wide range of reading and writing conferences, you'll also want to consider these practical, tried-and-true management tips.

Tips for Productive Student Conferences

- Explain the purpose of the conference.
- Demonstrate for the whole class, when necessary, how the conference works.
- Define your role and that of your students.
- Provide time to reflect on the process and outcomes.

Student Tips for Successful Writing Conferences

- Know the conference topic.
- Read the piece out loud to your partner or group.
- Point out what worked by using the topic, writing guidelines, and your partner's questions.
- Highlight needs by asking questions.
- Help your classmate note main points to use when revising.

Student Tips for Successful Reading Conferences

- Know the conference topic.
- Prepare by reading the material.
- Come to the conference with your book, a pencil, your reading log, journal, or conference form.
- Bring previous goals.
- Note and bring questions.

Some Ideas to Think About

Breaking away from 20-minute student-teacher conferences to brief, daily encounters enables you to clarify students' questions and pinpoint those who don't "get it." But you have to make sure you teach students how to confer in pairs and small groups. The time gained frees you to focus on students who need your support.

The checklist following helps me monitor how I integrate conferences into my daily schedule. You might want to periodically reflect on the list, then make adjustments.

Conference Reflection

Statement	Rarely	Sometimes	Always
I sit at my desk.			
I circulate around the room.			
I respond to students' names on the chalkboard.			
I identify student experts.			
I teach students how to confer.			
I encourage students to raise questions about their learning.			
I observe students at work.			
I use dated sticky notes for quick communication.			
I use a variety of conferences.			

Additional Notes:

CHAPTER 2

Whole-Group Conferences

G et your conference feet wet with whole-group conferences. You'll sharpen your kid-watching and note-taking skills while teaching students ways to reflect on reading and writing.

The Teacher-Observation Conference

T he purpose of this conference is to reinforce the productive behaviors you observe in students as they work in groups during writing and reading time. By sharing your observations and inviting students to share theirs, you all learn to identify what works and what needs improvement. To prepare for the conference, circulate, watch, listen, and take notes while students work independently. Decide on one area that could improve. Then, about 12 minutes before the end of the period, read notes and invite kids to discuss them. This conference is a great way to introduce and build the following conference skills:

✵ **LISTENING:** Students hear your observations.

✵ **NOTICING:** Students think about behaviors you've observed.

✵ **REFLECTING:** During discussions, kids reflect on their actions.

✵ **QUESTIONING:** Students can question your observations and the responses of classmates.

✵ **EVALUATING:** Students are asked to draw conclusions based on the teacher's observations and the follow-up class discussion.

✵ **SETTING GOALS:** Students help you set a goal they think they can meet the next time they work in groups on reading or writing.

A Teacher-Observation Conference in Action: Eighth Grade

Clipboard in hand, I circulate around the room, listening to and recording what's happening as my eighth graders, organized in groups of five, discuss *Cages, Earthquake*

Terror, Night of Fear, or *Nightmare Mountain,* all by Peg Kehret (Cobblehill).

About 15 minutes before the class ends, I ask students to wrap up their discussions and prepare for an observation conference. Using the overhead projector, I uncover one phrase at a time, read it, and elaborate on the notes so that students clearly understand my points. For example, for "Support proved it," I explain that two students complimented peers when they used specific examples from their books to show why a character was afraid.

NOTES ON GROUP BOOK-DISCUSSIONS
September 18, 1996

● all had books and response journals
● one student spoke at a time
● two students asked for proof from the book
● students read a section from the book
● "Support proved it."
● used quiet voices
● students on task the entire time

NEED: To value different interpretations and *politely* disagree.

All these comments highlighted what worked well. At first, students discussed all the positives. Several told exactly what they did. Here's how I moved them to reflect on a "need." →

Robb: You have a clear idea of what worked well today.

Matt: Don't forget to add that we stuck to what we were supposed to do.

Robb: Thanks for reminding me. That's an important observation. Now I want you to think about how you responded to classmates whose ideas differed from yours.

Sara: In our group, we asked them to show us support. [pause] But then some said the idea was dumb.

Tyler: We all got on Jamie when he disagreed with us. But he couldn't prove his point from the book.

Andy: I guess we could have just said we disagreed and not called his idea stupid. But it's hard to stay cool when you think you're right.

Robb: [I nod. Sometimes, when the truth comes out, it's better to listen and say little about students' remarks.] Any other comments? I heard lots of talk that told me we need to work on valuing others' ideas. How do you feel about that?

Anne: On our list of discussion guidelines, we agreed to be polite.

Robb: That's true, Anne. Does anyone have a suggestion for a goal we should set when we work in groups again?

At this point, the "need" was apparent to all. The class agreed, and we set a goal that I then added to the list of observations.

During the year, I repeat a teacher observation conference three to four times in the same learning situation. This allows me to show students' progress over time. The notes, taken during eighth-grade group book-discussions six weeks after my first observation conference, illustrate students' growth in accepting diverse ideas and

keeping a conversation going. Although students improved in several areas, their talk was so loud that it was difficult for groups to hear members.

NOTES ON GROUP BOOK-DISCUSSIONS
October 31, 1996

- all had books and journals
- many kept talk going and ask questions
- heard: "Anyone have a different idea?"
- students found implied meanings and used text
- all spoke
- laughter
- discussed questions
- groups set number of pages to read for Friday

NEED: To find a way to monitor and change noise levels.

I file the transparencies in a folder and make a photocopy of each. Such records support my memory of a class that occurred months ago. Moreover, students can review past observations, compare these to recent ones, and discuss growth and progress.

A Teacher-Observation Conference in Action: Fourth Grade

Sandy Palmer's fourth graders worked in small groups. Each group had selected and read a picture book and took turns giving summaries of it. They identified its genre, using examples from the book to make their point. Sandy's intent was that students learn how to summarize and to use the text to support their ideas.

Sandy moved from group to group, recording onto transparencies key phrases used by students. When the groups were finished, she gathered students on the rug and, placing her transparency on an overhead projector, spent 15 minutes reading her notes of things that students did well. As Sandy reads her notes, she expands them so fourth graders clearly understand each point. Sometimes Sandy records expanded notes during a planning period or after school. She keeps a photocopy of these dated transparencies in a folder so she can evaluate growth as the year progresses.

SOME OF SANDY PALMER'S NOTES AND EXPANDED COMMENTS
November 12, 1996
[Expanded comments are in italics.]

Elliot: used book to prove his point
Very nice job. You used your book to prove your point. Good readers and writers always prove their point with evidence. Good job!

Justin: good use of poetry vocab. : stanza
Your book was poetry, and I heard you use one of the poetry words—stanza. I'm glad to hear you using that word. Can you remind everyone what it means? [Justin tells the class.] Great!

LuisaAna: good summary of book
You did a nice job giving your brief summary without giving the ending away. Now others will be asking to read your book to find out how it ended!

Kayla: good use of criteria for poetry listed on chart
You were up against your whole group trying to prove to them that your book was poetry, weren't you? I was pleased to see you use the chart to help you!

Sandy chooses to record and share specific notes about each student. "Fourth graders benefit from individual comments because they don't always know which general statements apply to them," she said.

She wrapped up her teacher-observation conference by asking students if they'd like to respond to her comments. Sometimes students add observations she missed. "I also

T I P   B O X

Picture Book Practice

Picture books in fourth grade? Yes! Whenever I move students from practicing a reading strategy during guided practice to applying it on their own, I have them work with a thought-provoking picture book such as *Boundless Grace* by Mary Hoffman (Dial) and *The Freedom Riddle* retold by Angela Shelf Medearis (Lodestar). Picture books, which have all the elements of a story in a relatively condensed form, allow students to completely work through a strategy (predicting, summarizing, and so on) in one period. This, in turn, allows me to quickly evaluate whether or not they require additional guided practice or can move to using the strategy with their chapter books. I give students the opportunity to choose from among 30 books, which I display on a table. Then small groups of students take turns selecting one to work with during a 30–45 minute class period. First I name the strategy they will apply on their own. Then students and I review how the strategy works. After fielding questions, students independently apply the strategy using their picturebooks. Then they record written responses in their notebooks or on separate sheets of paper.

encourage students to compliment one another so they learn how to point out strengths during a conference," said Sandy.

A Tune-Up Two Weeks Later

A few weeks later, Sandy held another observation conference with her book-discussion groups. While membership had changed, students were still practicing the reading strategies of summarizing and using the text to support their ideas about genre. Between conferences, Sandy had modeled how she used these strategies, helping her students get the hang of proving an opinion with evidence from the book.

"Not everyone improves their use of the strategies," Sandy explained. "I don't expect that over a two-week period. But for the students who still struggle, I praise their progress in listening, using a quiet voice, showing illustrations so all members can see, and asking questions that help a classmate."

The Spotlighting Conference

In a spotlighting conference, I showcase one or two students who demonstrate an understanding of a reading or writing strategy introduced in mini-lessons.

During the last 15 minutes of class, these students have the "spotlight" and briefly explain how they approach a strategy such as note-taking. Then their classmates and I ask questions, clarifying the steps of the process so that they can "get it" too. Spotlight conferences are great for helping students see that are many ways to tackle a skill.

To keep track of who's been on center stage, I use a class list and grid. Each time I plan to spotlight, I explain that I'll try to select students who haven't had a turn.

Another benefit of spotlighting is that it gives me the chance to identify students who

---

TIP BOX

Ready, Get Set, Confer

If you're just starting with conferences, the teacher-observation conference is a good one to use first because it gives you the opportunity to observe everyone and sharpens your ability to objectively and briefly record students' behavior. Once you're comfortable with noting and sharing observations, implement spotlighting conferences. Debriefing conferences will naturally fall into place because you will have already encouraged students to think about their reading and writing.

"Spotlighting Conference" Record

Reading-Writing Workshop 8

	9/9	9/19	9/23	10/2	10/3	10/17	10/31	11/4	11/6	11/20	12/9	12/15
Robbie A.		✓								✓		
Tyler B.	✓											
Jamie C.				✓	✓					✓		
Sara D.		✓										
Matt F.							✓					
Anne G.	✓											
Wes H.								✓		✓		
Hunter K.						✓						
Andy L.							✓					
Sean R.										✓	✓	
Grayson S.							✓					

Keeping track of Spotlighting Conferences.

can support others. These peer coaches are a boon to me, as they can help out classmates when I'm busy.

A Spotlighting Conference in Action: Fifth Grade

As you will see, you don't pull the topic for a spotlighting conference out of thin air. This conference often follows on the heels of a mini-lesson when you realize kids aren't "getting it."

Let me share one of those moments: It was guided practice time; 20 fifth graders browsed through a bunch of picture books and chose a title to read and respond to during a guided practice session. (For more about guided practice, see page 59.)

I had placed three sticky notes in each book, one on the cover and two in the text, indicating where students were to stop, write a prediction, and offer detailed support for it from the title, the story, and the illustrations.

After reading their papers, I realized that most students did not offer specific examples from the text. The next day, I presented a mini-lesson on the difference between a general statement and detailed evidence. Using Elisa Bartone's *American Too* (Lothrop) as a model, I predicted what the book was about, using the title and cover illustration. First, I made general statements. Then I provided specific evidence so students could better understand the level of details I wanted.

GENERAL STATEMENTS

This book will be about a girl who comes from another country and wants to be an American.

SPECIFIC DETAILS

This book is about a young girl who is an Amercian and also has another heritage. The title, American Too, tells me that she is American and something else. The girl holds two flags—the American flag and one from another country.

Then I read the text, stopping to "think aloud" another prediction and to find support. I stopped where Rosie tells her brother Frankie not to come in her room. "Go away. This is a secret," she says. Again, I think aloud.

THINK-ALOUD WITH GENERAL STATEMENTS

Rosie's going to surprise everyone by doing what she wants.

THINK-ALOUD WITH SPECIFIC DETAILS

I remember Rosie being angry when her father told her she would be Queen of the feast of San Gennaro. Rosie thought that was too Italian and she wanted to be American. Maybe her surprise has to do with being American. [I tell students I need to look back for clues in the story and picture.] I show students the picture of the *Statue of Liberty*. I reread the text out loud—the part where Rosie wonders how she can really show she's American—her eyes look up just like the statue's eyes. The surprise is that Rosie will dress like the *Statue of Liberty* for the parade and be different from everyone.

In the discussion that followed my demonstration, students noticed the following:

☀ You really looked at the cover and found details.

☀ You thought about the title.

☀ You reread to find details.

☀ You didn't just trust your memory—you wanted to be exact.

☀ It took you time to find evidence.

After modeling, I suggested some questions students might ask themselves as they search for examples.

QUESTIONS FROM THE MINI-LESSON

☀ What words in the title supported your prediction?

☀ Which picture did you use, and what did you learn from each?

☀ What did the character do or say?

☀ Did other characters do or say things?

To find and add detailed examples to their support sections, I asked students to skim and reread parts of their books. That day I "spotlighted" Kim. Here's what she told her classmates:

First, I reread my predictions and support. Then I reread the book and I fixed what I had, but I added more examples for each support. I had to spend time on the pictures. I even skimmed the story to find details. I quoted some of the words.

A lively question-and-discussion period followed. One student asked, "Why did you quote words from the book?" And another wondered, "Why did you do all that rereading? Couldn't you just try to remember?"

From Kim, others learned that a quote really shows details because it's the exact words of a character or the author. For several minutes the entire class debated the benefits of rereading and skimming. Most agreed that "doing it that way" helped Kim find "very specific evidence for her predictions."

Words of advice from a peer are more apt to effect change than words from a teacher. Kim's success and her ability to explain why she would stick to rereading and skimming set many students on a course that went beyond "trying to remember."

The Debriefing Conference

In these 10- to 15-minute sessions, students publicize all the information they've learned about a reading or writing strategy. A natural time to hold one is when students have accrued enough experience to comfortably discuss what they've been learning. Debriefing topics can be as specific as a writing skill such as using punctuation in dialogue, or as general as what they learned in the course of writing a research paper.

Going public like this not only expands children's knowledge about how to tackle a certain issue but provides a safe forum to air what still confuses them.

Teach the Purpose of Debriefing

Help students understand their role during debriefings by explaining the purpose and your expectations. Here are some guidelines:

* Share thoughts without judging them right or wrong, good or bad.

* Emphasize strengths.

* Listen to others carefully, and raise questions about comments.

* Formulate a goal that will help you move forward as you continue to practice and apply what you're learning.

Pose Questions That Will Frame the Discussion

Before a debriefing, work with students to draft open-ended questions about the topic:

* Did you adapt or change the strategy or technique? How, and why?

* How did the strategy or technique help you with reading or writing?

* Think of three to four words that come to mind as you reflect on your process. Explain how each word relates to the strategy or technique.

* Did you experience confusion? When? What did you do?

Fifth graders, reflecting on their use of dialogue in their stories, posed the following questions:

* How did I show that the person talking changed?

* Did I use inner thoughts where the character was thinking to herself?

* How do inner thoughts show what a character is like?

* What do others learn about my characters from the dialogue?

I organized students into groups of three and invited groups to exchange ideas and offer examples from their work. Then the entire class shared their ideas and suggestions, and I recorded these on chart paper so we could review and revise them later.

Pinpoint Who Needs a Follow-Up Conference

Through this discussion, I can identify which students are not yet starting a new paragraph for each speaker in their story and can schedule a conference with them. Students who still need to learn how to add inner thoughts constitute another group.

You can either do these follow-up sessions right after the debriefing or at another time. For example, I could appoint two capable students to lead a session on writing inner thoughts while I work with those who still struggle with paragraphing dialogue. The rest of the class can work in pairs, read one another's pieces, or pose questions raised by the story and record them on sticky notes.

Use Debriefings to Discover Conference Topics and Organize Group Conferences

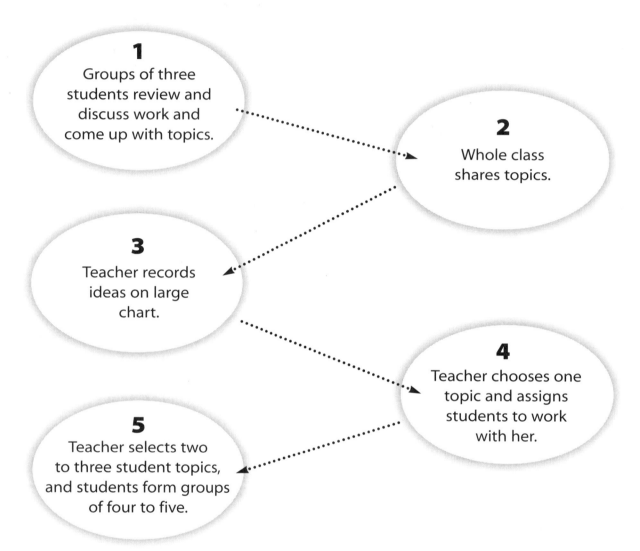

1
Groups of three students review and discuss work and come up with topics.

2
Whole class shares topics.

3
Teacher records ideas on large chart.

4
Teacher chooses one topic and assigns students to work with her.

5
Teacher selects two to three student topics, and students form groups of four to five.

Some Ideas to Think About

Now that you've successfully integrated some whole-group conferences into your classroom, you're ready to move on to implementing small-group conferences.

Reflect on the questions that follow. Your answers can help you decide where to begin:

- Do I frequently visit students throughout the day? (Try Making the Rounds Conferences.)

- Have I identified student experts who can help their classmates? (Try Partner Conferences.)

- Are there students who need individualized help to progress in reading and writing? (Try Focus Conferences.)

CHAPTER 3

Small-Group and Individual Conferences

Small-group conferences will provide an ever-useful forum for students to share ideas, but they succeed only after students have participated for some time in teacher-led conferences.

An effective way to model how partner and small-group conferences work is to create a demonstration theater. Onstage—at the front of the classroom—I confer with one student or a small group while the "audience" watches. Reserve time after the demonstration for the audience to ask questions and point out strengths and areas for improvement. Repeat these "onstage conferences" until you sense that students can work independently. What's the ideal number of small-group participants? I've found that pairs or groups of three or four students work best.

A Small-Group Conference in Action: Sixth Grade

At times, you can use small-group conferences to bandage and improve discussion group dynamics. For example, during bimonthly small-group book discussions, one group of sixth graders argued about selecting a group leader, engaged in social talk, and constantly interrupted one another. Close to the end of their second book discussion, I joined them and shared my observations. Comments such as "Not fair" and "We'll do it next time" rippled through the group.

A week before the third book discussion I scheduled two conferences with the derailed discussion group. At our first conference, I reviewed three behavior guidelines the class had set: 1) listen; 2) one person at a time talks; 3) value others' ideas. I promised to hold them to the standards they helped set. Then I suggested that they let chance decide the group leader for the next four book conversations. After numbering and folding four pieces of paper, I placed them in a box. Each student drew a folded paper and number one became the first group leader.

Our second conference opened with a review mini-lesson on how to take notes for a book discussion. With my guidance, students jotted in journals notes about their books.

After the third book discussion, while the rest of the class read or worked on writing, I helped the four conduct a debriefing conference. Students arrived at the following list of observations and a common goal:

✳ Now we know who is group leader for the next time.

✳ We can take turns and all get a chance [to be group leader].

✳ The notes helped me talk.

✳ We did talk about our books.

✳ After Shauna talked, I wanted to read Last Look (Clyde Robert Bulla, Puffin).

✳ We weren't the loudest group.

Goal: To prepare notes for the next talk and start without Mrs. Robb.

My interventions broke this group's negative cycle and jump-started these students into holding more successful book discussions.

A Partner Conference in Action: Seventh Grade

My seventh graders had been studying how authors use dialogue and descriptive details to reveal a character's personality. Students worked in pairs, reading one another's first drafts of character descriptions. I had not read their pieces. My goal for these partner conferences was for the students to learn how to help one another fine-tune their writing—before I read it.

I instructed partners to read each other's pieces silently and then take turns pointing out the places in their classmate's piece that show character traits. I asked them to make one to two suggestions that could improve the piece. Simon and Tywan read each other's stories silently. What follows is a transcription of Tywan's feedback to Simon. (Simon's story is about Jon, who is trying to get Amy to let him copy her math homework on the bus.)

Tywan: The details in the setting put me right on the school bus. I like when you had Jon think that he would sit near Amy because he knew she was smart. You helped me see Amy was nervous by showing her eye twitch and fingers tapping.

Simon: Do you think I had Jon ask for the work too fast?

Tywan: Yeah. I think you could have Jon be smoother and then move in. You know, get Amy off guard first.

Simon: [Jots down this suggestion on scrap paper.]

Tywan: Does Amy want to go out with Jon? Is she scared of him?

Simon: I'm not sure.

Tywan: Maybe you need to show why Amy gave in so fast. There's not enough to make me think she'd give him the homework to copy.

Simon: Where could I put that?

Tywan: Maybe when Jon sits down she could think something about him being popular and asking her to the movies and even that she thinks he's cool.

Simon: [takes notes] Now let's talk about yours.

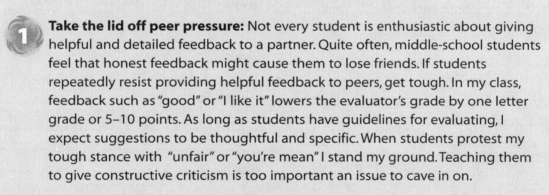

Avoiding Common Pitfalls of Peer Work

1 **Take the lid off peer pressure:** Not every student is enthusiastic about giving helpful and detailed feedback to a partner. Quite often, middle-school students feel that honest feedback might cause them to lose friends. If students repeatedly resist providing helpful feedback to peers, get tough. In my class, feedback such as "good" or "I like it" lowers the evaluator's grade by one letter grade or 5–10 points. As long as students have guidelines for evaluating, I expect suggestions to be thoughtful and specific. When students protest my tough stance with "unfair" or "you're mean" I stand my ground. Teaching them to give constructive criticism is too important an issue to cave in on.

2 **Clearly define the time:** Beyond the social roadblock, partner conferences can derail if you don't give students very clear guideposts stating the exact agenda for the conference and the evaluation tools you want them to use. When students say or write, "That was good," or "I enjoyed your story," they might not understand the purpose of the conference or have criteria to guide their evaluation. (See pages 107–108 for more about setting guidelines and evaluation.)

3 **Team up readers and writers who can help each other:** You also need to pair students who you know can give something to each other. When partner's expertise and experience are similar, each receives valuable advice. If you have a group of weak or struggling students, you should work with them one-on-one or in groups of two or three until they have progressed enough to peer-evaluate and provide helpful suggestions.

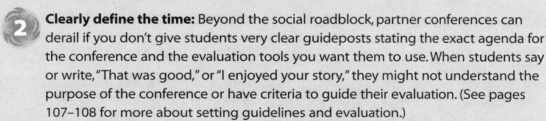

A Small-Group Conference in Action: Eighth Grade

Student-led conferences work well once students have conferred with their teacher and have a model to guide them. I cannot emphasize enough that clearly identifying the topic helps students focus and achieve success. The following discussion resulted from a student-led small-group conference that was tape-recorded.

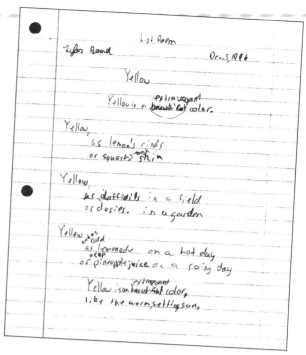

An eighth grader's list poem, with revisions.

TOPIC: Revising poems for verbs and specific nouns that create images

MATERIALS: Early drafts of poems

TIME: 15 minutes

STUDENTS: Sara (conference leader), Anne, Tyler, and Andy

Sara: How about circling all the verbs and underlining the nouns?

Anne: What if we can't find them?

Sara: We can help each other.

Andy: Should we do all? I have four poems.

Sara: Let's do one and see if there's time for more.

[They mark up one poem.]

Tyler: Okay, now what?

Anne: We can write other words in the margin or under the poem.

Tyler: [Students work silently for about 3 minutes.] Let's trade and see if we can add words to the lists.

[Students pass their poems around and jot down extra words. This takes about 5 minutes.]

Sara: Pick the word you think will be best and read it out loud.

Andy: To ourselves or to the group?

Sara: To the group—then we can give our opinion.

Individual Conferences:

The Making-the-Rounds Conference

Much like a doctor visits patients daily in the hospital, I circulate among students and chat for one to three minutes with individuals as they read, write, research, or work on a project. Through these visits I draw conclusions about their needs, monitor their goals, respond to questions, and offer support as they apply strategies and techniques observed during mini-lessons. I can also identify students who require more than a brief meeting and either assign a peer coach or set aside time for them to work with me. Peer coaches free me up to work with weaker students. Students should coach only if they are comfortable with that role and have a solid grasp of the specific topic. I

determine in advance, the times I will need these student experts and speak to them about their assigments to make sure they understand their task. Then part of our class becomes a 10-minute support session for all students—so I'm not asking anyone to miss their work on account of helping others.

The guidelines that follow will help you get started with this kind of conferring.

Advice That Sticks

For each conference, I jot down key pieces of the conversation on a sticky note, along with the date and the child's name. After we've talked, I give the student this note, attaching it to the page of writing he or she is working on. This way, students can reread and think about our exchange and apply it to their work. Students actually love these written reminders and often store them in their writing folders or reading-response journals.

A Making-the-Rounds Conference in Action: Fifth Grade

First, a bit of background so you can see the context for conferring: The students were

Guidelines for Making the Rounds

- **WATCH** the child. Begin by stating what you see.
- **WAIT** at least one minute for the student to say something.
- **HELP** the student find possible solutions.
- **INTERVENE** if you believe the student would benefit from support at this time.

writing fairy tales when I made the rounds, but they didn't just leap into writing them. I spent two weeks working with the class to establish content and mechanics criteria for a fairy tale. I opened each writing workshop by reading a fairy tale aloud. Students then read and discussed dozens of fairy tales in small groups. Using their experiences, students helped me create a list of fairy tale elements.

Then I asked each group to take 10–15 minutes to select five elements to include in their stories. I wrote each group's choices on the chalkboard. From that list, students selected four elements chosen by all groups. It took an additional five minutes for the class to agree on "happy ending" as the fifth element. Because students were writing in their fairy tale genre, I let them include more than the usual three content guidelines.

Students were also asked to add a mechanics skill from the list of "Skills I Have Learned" that they keep in their writing folders. We established the criteria before they began planning and drafting their fairy tales:

CONTENT CRITERIA
- a hero or heroine with one problem
- an evildoer
- tasks to perform to solve problem
- include magic number 3 and/or 7
- happy ending

MECHANICS CRITERIA
- complete sentences
- correct paragraphing
- use commas correctly (see chart)
- add a skill from your writing folder

By the time I made the rounds, my fifth graders had begun to work on original fairy tales, their heads full of ideas and clearly established guidelines.

After reviewing the criteria—something I do frequently—I announced that I would circulate around the room for the next 35 minutes and visit. "If you have a burning question," I told the class, "raise your hand and I'll pop over as quickly as I can." I always make sure students know they don't have to wait "forever" until I get to them.

Christian's and Pat's hands shot up. As I walked to Christian's desk, I assured Pat that I would visit with him in a few minutes.

I leaned down next to Christian's desk to make eye contact.

Christian: *Do I have to make a plan? I have all my ideas. [He shows me a long list of details.]*

Robb: *So you plan to use all of these?*

Christian: *No. [pause] I'm not sure.*

Robb: *Maybe the plan will help. Start by checking items you want to include. Then fill in your chart with the content criteria.*

Christian: *Can I do it with Jeff?*

Robb: *Sure. Try to have something to show by the end of class. [I give Christian a deadline to help him focus on his task.]*

I walked to Pat's desk and bent down next to him.

Robb: *I see that you are drawing pictures. Hmm. [I pick up paper.] This looks like it might be the evildoer in your story.*

Pat: *It is. He's going to hide the magic ring and turn the hero into an eagle. Can I draw pictures before I start writing? You okayed my plan.*

Robb: *Sure. That sounds like a great way to get to know your characters. You might* want to weave the pictures into your story. Look at Gordon's last story—he did that.

Pat: I'll look before I start writing. [She returns to drawing.] On a sticky note, I write a reminder to Pat to confer with Gordon this week. Then I stick the note above the evildoer's face.

As I circled the room, I thought about how important it is to allow kids to use visuals as an entrance into their stories.

I moved from group to group, making brief comments to students such as "The details in that plan will make your writing easier" or "I can't wait to read your story. The title 'Eagle Valley' intrigues me." Next, I visited with Leah who was staring at blank paper.

Robb: [gently] Can I help?

Leah: [after a long pause] I can't decide. I have two ideas. I don't know which one to do.

Robb: That's a great problem to have. How can you try to solve it?

Leah: I could talk to someone about it.

Robb: That's a good suggestion. But first, brainstorm lists for each idea and then find a partner to talk to. [I purposely ask Leah to get some ideas on paper. I want her to start thinking about both ideas before she talks to a partner. This will focus the talk.]

A Making-the-Rounds Conference in Action: Sixth Grade

Once each week, sixth graders and I work on poetry. We'd just completed a mini-lesson on giving shape to poems. After the demonstrations, groups practiced with poems I had rewritten as prose.

"Some of you might want to play with the shape of one of the poems in your folder," I told the class. "By play, I mean create different shapes until you find the one that works for your poem." Then I added, "If you're revising your lyric poem, continue with that."

First, I paused at Jennifer's desk. She'd chosen five small poems that she's been fine-tuning for three weeks and placed them across the desktop.

Robb: What are you planning to do with these?

Jennifer: I'm making a book of small poems. I want to think about the order I want them in. I'll do that and then shape each one.

Robb: You might want to shape first.

Jennifer: Why?

Robb: As you shape, you might revise an image or remove words. I'd think about order after you shape each one.

Jennifer: I'm happy with the way I shaped these [points to three poems]. I guess I'll work on both of these.

[I stick a note on her folder. The note suggests that Jennifer read the poems aloud and listen to how they sound as she tries to order them.]

I went to Ian's desk; he was reading.

Robb: What are you reading?

Ian: Celebrations by Myra Cohn Livingston.

Robb: Why are you reading those poems?

Ian: I want to look at ways poets shape theirs before I start mine. I might read some other books.

Robb: Good idea. But remember, the deadline

for complete revisions of one poem—and that includes shaping—is in four days.

Ian: I'll make it. [I pat Ian on the back and move on.]

Shelley's hand went up.

Robb: How can I help?

Shelley: I want to make my poem about a scallop shell look like one. But all my shells look like weird circles.

Robb: Who do you think can help you?

Shelley: Can I ask Charlie to draw a shell for me?

Robb: Looks like Charlie is working on his poem. You can ask him to give you time tomorrow and work on another poem now.

Shelley: Can I go to the library and find a book with pictures of shells?

Robb: Sure. Check the book out and bring it back to class.

And so I continued chatting with students. My goal is to help them solve problems that arise, to keep them writing and thinking, and to note which students require additional help. For example, during that period, Chris said that he liked his poem's shape and didn't want to change it. I spent a few extra minutes with Chris and gave him a jump start by reshaping the first three lines of his poem. "I can do it," he grumbled impatiently. Pencil in hand, he began to work. That was my goal.

A Making-the-Rounds Conference in Action: Eighth Grade

During reading-writing workshop, 11 students were reading their library books, 7 were drafting or revising pieces, 3 worked on independent research projects, and 2 were improving their predict/support/confirm or adjust paper.

I announced that for the next 40 minutes, I'd circulate and visit as many students as possible. Some students only needed a pat on the back or a comment such as "Looks like you're really into revising the lead of your story." A nod or no response let me know that the student was deep in thought and that this was not the time to chat.

I moved on to Maria. Instead of reading, she was staring at the ceiling.

Robb: How are things going?

Maria: I don't like this book. I've read half of it. I want to change, but I don't think I can finish a new one and meet our group's deadline.

Robb: I think it's important to read a book you really like.

[On a sticky note, I write three titles: The Journey Back by Johanna Reiss (HarperCollins), Nightfather by Carl Friedman, (Sundance), and The Shadow Children by Steven Schnur (Morrow).]

See if you like any of these. If not, ask Mrs. Wheeler, the librarian, to help you.

Maria: What about the group?

Robb: Call a meeting 10 minutes before class ends and negotiate an extra week. No one will turn down extra time.

Next, I visited Albert, who was revising his prediction work.

Robb: I see that you're rereading the story.

Albert: Yeah. What else can I do?

Robb: You can skim to the first "Stop and Predict" and only reread the sections that have the details for your prediction. [I jot this on a sticky note, attach it to Albert's paper, and stay a few minutes, watching him skim the first part.]

Anne raised her hand; I climbed over two book bags to her table.

Robb: How can I help?

Anne: I forgot how to set up the dialogue. [She shows me half a page of her rewrite of the dialogue in her story—no paragraphing with each new speaker.]

Robb: How can you refresh your memory?

Anne: My journal's at home. I don't have the examples. Umm. [pause] I could look at the chart the class wrote. But I'd rather get Missy to help.

Robb: Missy's in the library. Using the chart's a good idea. Look at what happens every time the speaker changes. [I write the following on a sticky note and place it on Anne's first draft: "Every time the speaker changes, start a new paragraph."]

As I walked toward Michael, I wrote myself a reminder: Tomorrow have a focus conference with Anne.

The Focus Conference

This 5–10-minute conference is designed to zero in on one issue raised by you or the student. I've found that students feel more secure with this limited focus. As a sixth grader wrote in a self-evaluation, "I can think about and make one thing better. If I have to work on five things at once, forget it."

Focus conferences can take place during reading-writing workshop when students work independently. You can easily meet with four to five students each day and still have time for other class projects. You can call them, or students can request them.

During a focus conference I can bandage a student's problem, by listening, offering practical strategies, and watching the child use a strategy. It's the extra time I have for watching that makes this such a valuable

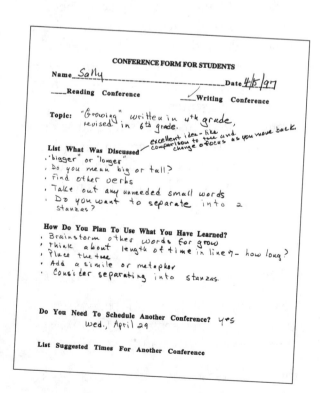

During a conference, a sixth grader decides what to revise.

conference. At that point, I decide whether a child can successfully work alone or with a group, or whether I want to schedule a longer conference.

I record students' comments and mine on a form like the one shown on page 41. Students store these notes in a writing folder, journal, or book. The notes are available to students when they revise a piece of writing, respond to a book, or apply a reading strategy.

A Focus Conference in Action: Fourth Grade

Fourth graders are famous for starting every sentence with the same word or phrase—for example, *Another, Then, And then*. Or they omit these connecting words and their paragraphs become one long sentence.

After presenting several mini-lessons on ways to kick this habit, I asked students to select a piece of writing, circle all of the *And then*'s and *Then*'s, and mark places where these words could be deleted. I also pointed to the chalkboard and read aloud a list of alternatives: *after that, afterward, next, later on, next time, finally*. Students got to work repairing their sentences.

But I noticed that Max struggled as he tried to fix his work. He got up out of his seat and printed his name in large letters under "Right Now." I headed over to his desk immediately.

Max: I can't fix these so they make sense.

Robb: Can you tell me what the problem is?

Max: I only have one period for ten lines. I haven't marked any sentences. I just wrote what came into my head.

Robb: Read your piece aloud and circle all of the repeated words we talked about during the mini-lesson.

[Max completes this task.]

Robb: Good job! Now reread and mark the beginnings and ends of sentences. When you pause to breathe and when you change to a different idea, think about starting a new sentence.

[Max successfully completes this task.]

Max: What if I want to keep some of those words?

Robb: You can keep one or two. You might find you don't need those words at the start of your sentence. If you do, then try to use one of the words on the chalkboard.

Getting Unstuck

I praised Max because he asked for help immediately instead of stewing and growing frustrated. High on my agenda is to encourage students to feel free to get help quickly. In time, students become skilled at recognizing when peer help will suffice, when they should figure it out for themselves, and when they need my support to—as one child put it—"get unstuck."

A Focus Conference in Action: Fifth Grade

TOPIC: Finding clues to figure out the meaning of an unknown word

BOOK: *The Not So Jolly Roger* by Jon Scieszka (Puffin)

TIME: 8 minutes

Marcia has read the first three chapters and identified on a sticky note one word she still doesn't understand. Marcia called the conference.

She sits with me at the conference table in one corner of the room.

Robb: How do you like your book?

Marcia: It's great. This is my third Time Warp Trio book, and next I'm going to read the new one, Tut, Tut.

Robb: Sounds like you're having a great time with these books.

Marcia: Jon Scieszka's my all-time favorite author.

Robb: He makes me laugh. I can understand why you like his books so much.

Marcia: I need you to help me with a word. There were no clues in the sentence. I figured out bristled [page 12] because it said "out front" at the end of the sentence.

Robb: You used the clue in the sentence well.

Marcia: I had trouble with executed. [She opens her book to page 8.] There aren't any clues—even to the end of the page.

Robb: Read the top of page 9 to yourself a

few times. See if you find clues there.

Marcia: But you said clues were close to the word.

Robb: That's true. But sometimes you have to read on. You might even have to back up and read what came before the word. [Sandra reads silently.]

Marcia: Maybe it means getting shot and stabbed by pirates. I think that's what it is. If they steal the treasure, pirates will get back at them that way.

Robb: Good job. Next time you need help figuring out a word, I think you and your reading buddy can do a great job.

The Solo Conference

Ultimately, the goal of all of these classroom conferences is to provide students with methods of reflection that they can use by themselves, for themselves. Conferences with others are the training ground for conferring with yourself. As children talk and consider possible solutions for various reading and writing issues, they learn to apply specific strategies to their work—proofreading to catch spelling errors, predicting to improve reading comprehension, and the like—but more importantly, they exercise self-evaluative thinking, which will serve them well in every arena. Labeling it a "solo" conference or a "self conference" is simply a way of letting children know that you value this opportunity to think things through and to fix things independently.

A Solo-Conference in Action: Fifth Grade

As with other sections of this book, I want to provide some background information that led to this particular set of solo conferences so that you can "taste all the ingredients" that are involved:

For three months, fifth graders drafted and revised their memoirs. In addition to doing a series of memoir-craft mini-lessons, students and I examined powerful memoirs such as *Through Grandpa's Eyes* by Patricia MacLachlan (HarperCollins), *Boy* by Roald Dahl (Puffin), *Hey World, Here I Am!* by Jean Little (HarperCollins), Tomi dePaola's *Now One Foot, Now the Other* (Putnam), *Nana Upstairs & Nana Downstairs* (Viking), and *The Art Lesson* (Putnam). Before diving into the writing, students and I set these content guidelines:

1. Stick to one memory. Have notes and a writing plan.
2. Write a lead that hooks the reader.
3. Show with details, don't tell.
4. Use verbs that paint pictures.

Throughout the three-month period, students and I negotiated deadlines for collecting ideas, creating a writing plan, drafting, and revising.

I also asked students to self-evaluate their memoir-in-progress, even before they turned in their writing plan. I first modeled a self-evaluation using examples from my own memoir. I wanted children to know exactly how to check their writing against each content guideline.

Writing Plans

Writing plans guide writers just as road maps guide drivers. Plans invite students to think about, select, and organize their ideas before drafting. They can be a list, a web of ideas, a drawing, or an outline.

A fourth grader plans the three parts of her story with a web.

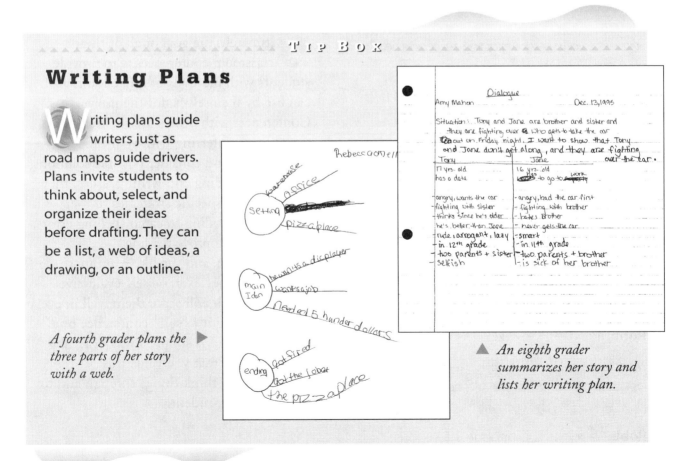

An eighth grader summarizes her story and lists her writing plan.

Laura Robb's Written Self-Evaluation of Her Memoir

After I finished my draft, I reread my lead: "Eyes wide open, I lay in bed. Soon, I thought, I would to go down to the kitchen." After writing three other leads I chose this one: " 'Lights out,' " said mom. I shut my reading lamp, snuggled under my covers, and waited." It was better because the reader now knows I'm waiting for something. This one would make the reader continue. I circled three verbs to change—*went, tasted,* and *took*—and changed these to *crept, licked,* and *grabbed.* In one place, I told how I felt instead of showing I was ashamed that I snuck the candy and ate it. I changed that to "I breathed quickly and my cheeks burned. The hot, flushed feeling didn't stop me from stuffing chocolates into my mouth."

Most students didn't think that they could write such a detailed paragraph as I had. To support them, I wrote on chart paper these instructions (which refer to the content guidelines on previous page):

1. Have the four guidelines on your desk.
2. Reread your memoir.
3. Write a paragraph similar to the one I modeled.
4. Start with the first guideline, and write about it. Tell what kind of writing plan you developed.
5. Comment on your first and revised leads.
6. Include a passage in which you showed and didn't tell.
7. Write about two to three verbs you changed.

Students always write their self-evaluations during writing workshop beause I'm there to answer questions and give weaker students a jump-start if they need one.

Jose opened his self-evaluation with: "I did not try to write more leads. I know I'll stick with this one. 'Thick clouds filled with dark spirits were in the sky.' "

How surprised Jose was when, a few days later, he revised his lead to read "Dark clouds, like evil pirate ships, sailed across the sky."

"I need to find verbs for the four I circled," Deena wrote in her self-evaluation. Then she returned to her story and wrote two or three alternate verbs in the margins. Next, she replaced those she had circled with one of her alternates.

When students self-evaluate between their first and second draft, there's a bonus for me: The pieces I read are in such good shape, I don't have to spend as much time coaching them.

Fifth-grader Megan's revision plans, alternate leads, and her self-evaluation illustrate her progress in being able to reflect on revisions and set beneficial goals.

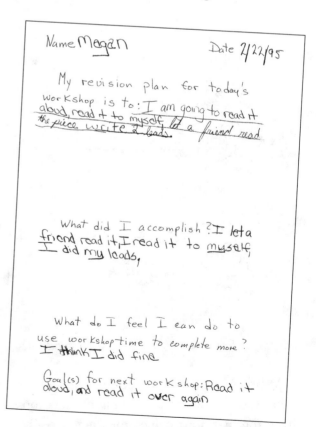

Megan's self-evaluation of a workshop session.

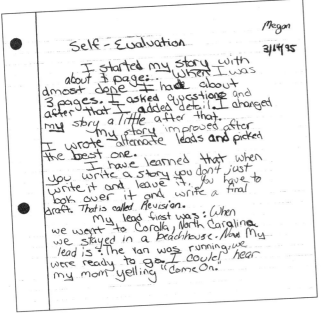

Megan writes alternate leads.

Megan chooses the lead for her piece.

Megan's self-evaluation based on writing guidelines.

When Megan turned her work in, she said, "Going back and checking my revisions from the first draft helped me know I really improved."

Use Peer Checkpoints Before Kids Write Final Drafts

Before my eighth graders attend to a polished draft, I have them find a partner to write an evaluation of their work. I create a peer evaluation sheet, like the one directly below, that includes established content criteria. Partners read each other's work and complete the evaluation form. Students staple peer evaluations to their writing, and I read the draft and the peer evaluation. On a sticky note, I applaud peers' suggestions, and if necessary add some of my own.

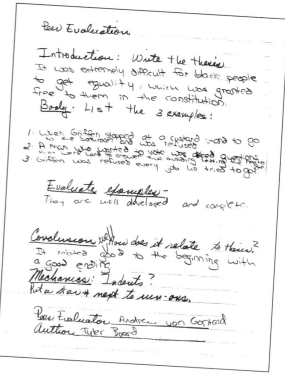

An eighth grade peer evaluation.

Tyler lists his revision goals.

After students read feedback from their partner and me, they list on scrap paper the revisions they plan to make (see illustration, page 45). Then students turn in final drafts in addition to early drafts and evaluations. Because I look at their process and progress from start to finish, assigning a grade is easy.

A Look at a Year's Conference Schedule

Integrating conferences into your teaching year is not difficult as long as you recognize up front that you can't and shouldn't do all of them. Some conferences, such as the teacher observation, debriefing, and parent-teacher conferences, occur periodically. Other conferences, such as making-the-rounds and focus conferences, become an almost daily event in a reading and writing workshop.

What follows is a conference schedule geared for teachers with one to three years classroom experience.

Suggested Reading and Writing Conference Schedule for New Teachers

SEPTEMBER

- Collect background data about students' reading and writing lives from parents and students.
- Teacher-Observation Conference
- Making the Rounds

OCTOBER

- Making the Rounds
- Focus Conference
- Teacher-Led Group-Share Writing Conference
- Teacher-Led Book Conference
- School-Scheduled Parent-Teacher Conference
- Second- and third-year teachers can start scheduling traditional reading and writing conferences to discuss collected background data—these will run through November.

NOVEMBER/DECEMBER

- Teacher-Observation Conference
- Making the Rounds
- Focus Conference
- Teacher-Led Group-Share Writing Conference
- Teacher-Led Book Conference
- Debriefing Conference

JANUARY

- Making the Rounds
- Focus Conference
- Teacher-Led Group-Share Writing Conference
- Teacher-Led Book Conference
- Debriefing Conference
- Spotlighting Conference
- Teacher-Led Small-Group Conference

FEBRUARY

- Teacher-Observation Conference
- Making the Rounds
- Focus Conference
- Spotlighting Conference
- Teacher-Led Group-Share Writing Conference
- Teacher-Led Book Conference

MARCH

- Making the Rounds
- Focus Conference
- Teacher-Led Group-Share Writing Conference
- Teacher-Led Book Conference
- Student-Led Partner or Group Conference
- School-Scheduled Parent-Teacher Conference (including child)

APRIL

- Teacher-Observation Conference
- Making the Rounds
- Focus Conference
- Spotlighting Conference
- Teacher-Led Group-Share Writing Conference
- Teacher-Led Book Conference
- Student-Led Partner or Group Conference
- Debriefing Conference

MAY/JUNE

- Making the Rounds
- Focus Conference
- Teacher-Led Group-Share Writing Conference
- Teacher-Led Book Conference
- Student-Led Partner or Group Conference
- Debriefing Conference

How's It Going?

Three to four months into the year, I organize students in groups, and ask them to discuss and note the benefits of the different types of conferences they've experienced. Here's a list composed by fourth and fifth graders. The type of conference they refer to is in parentheses:

☀ I get help right away. (Making the Rounds)

☀ I can see how others do it [solve the same problem]. (Spotlighting and Small-Group Conferences)

☀ When you tell us what we did that was great in discussion groups, it makes us feel good. Then it's easy to work on one thing we need to improve. (Teacher-Observation Conference)

☀ When I need more than a real short one, I don't have to wait a week. (Five-minute focused conference)

☀ Debriefings let me see what others do. (Debriefing Conference)

Students' reactions are my barometer for adjusting and planning the ways I use conferences.

Some Ideas to Think About

Near the end of October and again at the beginning of March, I evaluate the role that conferring plays in my classroom routines. Below are the questions I think about. Reflecting on them jogs my memory and nudges me to continuously model and follow through.

TEACHER'S QUESTIONS

● What kinds of conferences have I introduced?

● Do students understand the purpose of each conference?

● Have I modeled enough for students to meet without me?

● Am I watching and listening to students?

● Have I identified and used student experts?

● Do I confer with other teachers? Parents?

● Are students learning to hold a conference with parents and me?

● Have I reserved time for debriefings?

● Am I repeating observation conferences so that students and I can evaluate growth and needs?

CHAPTER 4

Finding Topics for Reading Conferences

Fifth-grader Kiesha and her family moved into Clarke County, Virginia, in February, joining a class during midyear at the elementary school. When she arrived, her new classmates were in the midst of a unit on the Middle Ages and were reading *The Door in the Wall* by Marguerite deAngeli. The teacher gave Kiesha a copy of the book and assured her that she would love it. But several days later Kiesha told her teacher, "The book's boring. I don't know anything about monks and monasteries or the Middle Ages."

Unlike her classmates, who had been immersed in this historical period, Kiesha found the book impenetrable. "I just can't connect to anything," she confessed. She remained silent during book discussions.

"I should have conferred with Kiesha to find out what she knew about the Middle Ages," her teacher told me when we talked one afternoon. "I'd have given her materials that would build her background knowledge about this period before giving her the novel." How right this teacher was! Perhaps now more than ever—with classrooms full of students with dramatically different life experiences and reading levels—it's essential for us to watch and confer with every child to determine their reading strengths and pinpoint areas where they need support.

Conferences are a great time to come to know who our students are and what they know. So often it's the personal background material—discovering that Sue is mad for horses and that Nathan will inhale any reading material about airplanes—that gives us insight into resolving a child's reading difficulty.

The Reading Survey: How Students See Themselves as Readers

Early in the school year, find out how students view themselves as readers by using the Reading Survey and the Seven Questions About Reading. Having students write about their school and home reading lives will prepare you for your first reading conference. Armed with information, you'll be able to confer about:

☀ the authors and books students enjoy.

☀ books you recommend.

☀ reasonable goals to set for the first weeks of school.

☀ the strengths and needs of each student.

☀ reading strategies that students understand and use.

TIP BOX

Seven Questions About Reading: Modeling Makes a Difference

Before setting students to work answering the seven questions, take three days and model how *you* would answer them. Showing students how you do it will result in more thorough and thoughtful student writing. They'll also learn about your reading life.

On the first day, using a colored marker, write the questions on chart paper and leave room between each for notes. Think aloud, explaining how you would respond to each question. Jot down notes in a different-colored marker. On the second day, reread your notes and add new ideas. On the third day, use your notes to write your final responses on chart paper. Hang the charts so that students have a model to follow.

Students can respond to each question by writing a separate paragraph, or they can respond number by number. For the Seven Questions, see page 53.

Reading Survey

Name _____ **Date** _____

Fill in the blanks.

1. What words pop into your mind when you think of reading a book?

_____

2. Do you read at home?_____ How often do you read at home? _____

3. Where's your favorite place to read at home?_____ At school?_____

4. How do you find books you love to read?_____

5. Besides books, what other types of materials do you read? _____

_____ Why do you enjoy these?_____

6. Do you own a library card?_____ How often do you visit the library to check out books?

_____

Complete these sentences.

7. My favorite author is _____.

8. The best book I read is _____.

9. The best book someone read to me is _____.

10. The topics I enjoy reading about are _____.

11. I watch TV for _____ hours a day because _____.

12. The things I'm great at as a reader are _____.

13. Things I need to work on to improve my reading are _____.

14. I use these strategies as I read: _____.

15. I enjoy talking about books because _____.

16. I enjoy writing about books because _____.

Reading Survey (Top)

Name Andy Lowder Date Sept 1996

Fill in the blanks.

1. What words pop into your mind when you think of reading a book?
hate boring bad sleep hard

2. Do you read at home? NO How often do you read at home? _____
_____

3. Where's your favorite place to read at home? _____
At school? sit on a bean bag

4. How do you find books you love to read? I dont pick
books out by myself.

5. Besides books, what other types of materials do you read? Magazines
on skating and skiing Why do you enjoy these? Lix sports-Fast read

6. Do you own a library card? Moms How often do you visit the library to
check out books? Only when I haft to

Complete these sentences.

7. My favorite author is Gary Paulsen

8. The best book I read is Hatchet

9. The best book someone read to me is Nightmare Mountain

10. The topics I enjoy reading about are Sports

11. I watch TV for 1 hours a day because I like the
Simpsons

12. The things I'm great at as a reader are nothing

13. Things I need to work on to improve my reading are read faster,
finding books to read that I can read.

14. I use these strategies as I read none

15. I enjoy talking about books because no

16. I enjoy writing about books because no

Reading Survey (Bottom)

Name Andy Lowder Date May 1997
Fill in the blanks.

1. What words pop into your mind when you think of reading a book?
easier, some are fun, space time

2. Do you read at home? yes How often do you read at home? every
day - 20 min.

3. Where's your favorite place to read at home? bed
At school? beanbag

4. How do you find books you love to read? I pick them out,
Ask teacher and Librarian

5. Besides books, what other types of materials do you read? mag.
_____ Why do you enjoy these? Fast read

6. Do you own a library card? moms How often do you visit the library to
check out books? Use school library alot

Complete these sentences.

7. My favorite author is Peg Kehret

8. The best book I read is Night of Fear

9. The best book someone read to me is Moves Make the Man

10. The topics I enjoy reading about are adventure - suspense - mystery

11. I watch TV for 1 hours a day because I have nothing
else to do

12. The things I'm great at as a reader are Predicting - Finding
support from book, making pictures in my head
adjusting predictions

13. Things I need to work on to improve my reading are Faster -
improve vocab. keep reading every night

14. I use these strategies as I read predict question make
pictures - skim

15. I enjoy talking about books because I remember what I read

16. I enjoy writing about books because it makes me
think about problems and characters

Eighth-grader Andy completes a reading survey at the beginning and end of the school year (see left). Andy prepares for a focus conference by reviewing his answers and reflecting on his progress. "I have strategies," he tells me, "and I've read more than 15 books. And my mom doesn't have to nag me to read."

Seven Questions About Reading

1 Why do you read?

2 What does reading mean to you? What benefits do you see in reading?

3 How do you think reading helps you?

4 Do you read at home? How often? What do you read?

5 What do you do well as a reader?

6 What are some of your favorite books? Why did you like them?

7 Do you have a favorite author? Why do you enjoy this author's books?

Some children will answer every question; others will not. Failure to answer a question is as significant as providing a detailed response. My job is to find out why students omit a question.

Andy's Reading Survey at the start of school. (Top left) Note the development Andy conveys in this survey, completed in May.

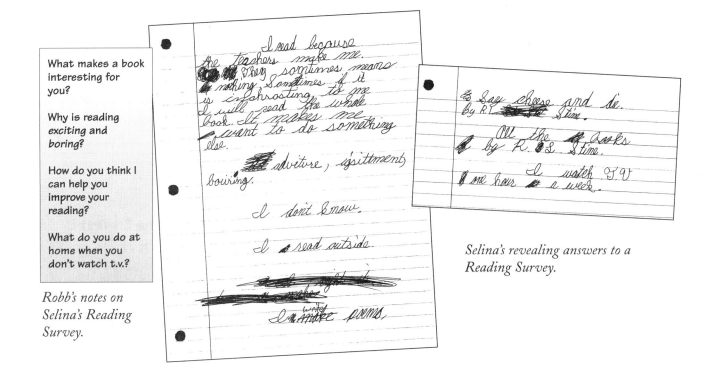

Robb's notes on Selina's Reading Survey.

Selina's revealing answers to a Reading Survey.

Fifth-grader Selina's answers (shown above) let me know exactly how she feels about reading. She reads because teachers make her.

Skills and Strategies: What's the Difference?

For me, a reading skill represents one stage of development and a strategy another. Both are related because both are helpful tools that can improve students' reading. Some examples of skills and strategies include figuring out unknown words in context, making sense of passages that confuse, recalling information, and making inferences. A skill becomes a strategy once the learner understands it and can apply it independently to new reading material.

Yet some books are interesting enough that Selina reads the entire text. These comments, plus her listing of R. L. Stine as her favorite author, provide me with a positive opening during a reading conference.

Even in a conference, Selina was unable to verbalize any of her reading strengths or the strategies she used. "Most of the books we read for school," she told me, "are too hard. I don't remember anything I read from them. So now I just don't read." Selina reads two years below grade level and constantly struggles with books she can't comprehend. For Selina to improve and change her attitude, she needs to learn from books that she can understand.

Over several months, Selina's teacher and I plan a variety of interventions to discuss with Selina during focus conferences and a few longer conferences. Here is a list of some of the things we addressed:

- ☀ Five-finger method of choosing a book

- ☀ Strategies for saying multisyllable words

- ☀ Predict/Support/Confirm/Adjust

- ☀ Repeated readings to develop fluency and comprehension

- ☀ Paired reading with a partner

- ☀ Visualizing characters and places

- ☀ Retellings

- ☀ Think-alouds: Selina read a passage and thought aloud, explaining what the passage meant and raising questions about confusing parts.

We encouraged Selina to reflect on how these strategies helped her, and we pointed out every inch of progress we observed.

As I read responses to the Seven Questions About Reading (see page 53), I jot down on sticky notes each student's strengths, needs, and any questions to raise in a reading conference. The notes for Selina's responses (see page 54) and Jennifer, a sixth-grader (see right) illustrate how much students reveal about themselves when they have time to explore the reading skills, strategies, and attitudes they bring to class.

Robb's Sticky Note Reactions

Note: Compliment honesty and ability to explain feelings.

● How has reading skill improved in the last 2 years?

● What do you think about when you "read words" but don't recall?

● What do you prefer to do instead of reading?

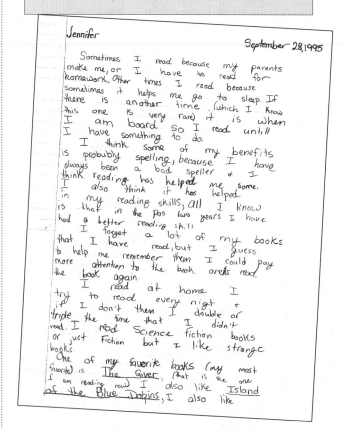

Jennifer's answers to the Seven Questions.

TIP BOX

Turn Skills Into Strategies

You can help move skills to the level of strategies by setting aside time for students to practice skills and offering opportunities for students to apply strategies to their independent reading. Schedule two periods each week for these guided practice sessions. For more about implementing guided practice sessions, see page 59.

Uncovering Conference Topics: General Tips

You will find topics for reading conferences within all of the watching, listening, and interacting with students that you do in the course of the school day. The list that follows outlines some of the criteria I use to select reading topics.

✓ **ASSESS WHAT STUDENTS ALREADY KNOW:** Discover what students know and don't know about a topic, a reading skill, or a strategy.

✓ **OBSERVE DURING GUIDED PRACTICE:** When students practice a reading strategy with the class or in small groups, note the questions they pose, where they seem to hesitate, and how they apply a strategy to the book they're reading.

✓ **LISTEN DURING BOOK DISCUSSIONS:** Discover what students recall, what they comprehend, and how they use facts to draw conclusions.

✓ **WATCH DURING INDEPENDENT READING:** During sustained silent reading time, invite a student to read a brief passage aloud. Listen for strengths and trouble spots. Ask if you can glance at their reading logs and review the kinds of books they select.

✓ **REVIEW RESPONSE JOURNALS:** Read entries and learn how students use stories and information to retell, summarize, think critically, draw conclusions, and support predictions.

✓ **ASSIGN STUDENTS SELF-EVALUATIONS:** Invite students to reflect on and then write about their feelings toward reading and the strategies they use as they read.

Uncovering Conference Topics in Prereading Activities

As you know, assessing a student's prior knowledge about a topic before giving the child a book about that topic is essential. The more kids know about a topic or concept before reading, the greater the recall and comprehension. But it's equally important to learn about children's *attitudes* toward reading and the skills and strategies they bring to your class. This prereading detective work on your part will give you clues as to what would make a meaningful conference topic for each student. Beyond having children fill out the Reading Survey and Seven Questions About Reading (see pages 52–53), here are some other ways to find topics for individual or group conferences.

Monitor Sharing Time

When children share what they think they know about a topic or predict what they believe a book will be about, I listen and take notes on the class roster sheet pinned to my clipboard. In my class, if a student doesn't want to share, he can say "Pass." So when a child continually passes over the course of five to six days, even though they are in a safe classroom environment, I literally take note and set up a focus conference with that child. I gently ask the student, "Why do you always choose to pass when the class exchanges ideas?" Here are excerpts of such conversations with students from various grades:

Dan: I hate to share. Everyone laughs at what I say. I'm always saying something dumb—like when the topic was snakes—I said "lasso." But I never said that I got it from Steven Kellogg's "Pecos Bill." I just stopped talking when the laughing started. (Grade 4)

Robb: I wish you had continued. Your idea showed a terrific connection. Next time, when you know your idea is solid, try taking a chance— you might find the laughter will quickly stop.

Jay: I don't want to talk in class. My voice is changing and it does weird things. (Grade 7)

Robb: I understand how you feel. Try to remember that the other boys are experiencing voice changes. We need your input. Think about it and I'll call on you only if your hand is up.

Gail: My ideas were said by others. By the time you get to me, I don't have anything else to say. (Grade 5)

Robb: [I'm thinking that Gail passes even when she's the second or third student to share, but I don't want to be confrontational.] Would you be comfortable raising your hand when you want me to begin the sharing with you? [She nods and I make note of her response so that I'll remember to watch for her hand.]

Jake: Brainstorming is dumb. It's a waste of time. I can't read the book my group has anyway, so why bother to do prereading stuff? (Grade 8)

Robb: I can help you find a book you can read. But before you change titles, let's confer the last 10 minutes of class. [During this time, students will be reading silently and I can listen to Jake read.]

Jake: Okay. But I hate reading. [pause] It's boring.

Robb: I can see that reading really upsets you. Let's talk about it more when we meet.

Most students' responses are like the first three—their roadblocks are easy to work through. The eighth grader's angry words, however, send a message about reading that must be investigated in a longer conference. Every time I pinpoint a child whose comments signal a reading difficulty, I recognize the value of these conferences, and of recording students' oral-response patterns with detailed notes.

Look at Reading-Journal Entries

Besides glancing over each one of your students' prereading entries to determine their prior kowledge, it's a good idea to periodically review a series of three to four entries. Reviewing a series of entries allows you to evaluate students' progress in generating ideas before reading a book, story, or textbook chapter, or before studying a theme or a topic. This will help you pinpoint what kids know about a topic or concept. In a sixth-grade class, I did this as I circulated, marking my class roster with a check to note progress and a dash to highlight students I wanted to confer with. These students wrote just two to three words and did not take any notes when the class shared ideas. The majority of students in this class didn't need a conference. On their journals I placed a sticky note that celebrated their progress. That day I conferred with the five students whose work showed no progress in recording ideas. Here's what one student said during this conference:

Millie: I don't write my ideas—they're probably dumb.

Robb: Your comments during discussions show good thinking.

Millie: I talk better than I write. My head is blank when I write.

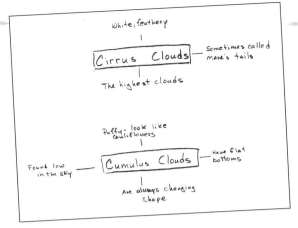

A class of fourth graders discussed two cloud webs.

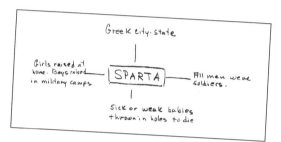

A web on Sparta that fifth graders discussed.

Robb: I think that you're censoring your ideas. Try to talk softly to yourself and write what you say.

Millie: Kids will think I'm weird.

Robb: Then say your idea to yourself—silently.

[To get Millie started the next time the class brainstorms, I have her dictate her ideas to me. I make sure I help Millie after I use the same technique with another student. I don't want Millie to feel she is the only one receiving this kind of support.]

Use a Web to Uncover Conference Topics

Discussing a web with children is another effective way to find those kids who need a special conference with you to shore up their lack of knowledge about a topic.

Write the topic in the center of a large sheet of chart paper. In the samples in the right column, fourth-grade teacher Heather Campbell focused on "Clouds," while I webbed the topic of "Sparta" with my fifth

graders. Branching out from the central word, we wrote five or six statements that reflect key concepts about the topic.

We then covered the statements with index cards by taping the top of the card to the chart. Flipping up one card at a time, we invited students to talk about each sentence or phrase.

Evaluate Prereading Entries

Before inviting students to write what they know about a topic, organize them into pairs or groups of four. Have students talk for two to three minutes about the topic. Next, ask all students to record their thoughts on a journal page, and then draw a line across the page directly under their last note. Students can add notes, based on whole-class discussion, below the line.

Note: When you review a series of entries, everything above the line represents ideas generated by the student; everything below the line represents the extra ideas students noted during a group-share session.

This journal entry shows a student's ideas above the line and class notes below it. ▶

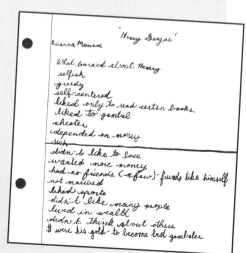

Discovering Conference Topics During Guided Practice

Before describing how to find conference topics during guided practice, I'd like to cover its basic tenets. Guided practice is the "bricks and mortar" of any reading program, and yet there's a lot of confusion about what the term means.

What Is Guided Practice?

Guided-practice sessions, 20–30-minute periods, are usually scheduled two times a week, during which teachers isolate a key reading strategy and demonstrate how it works. For example, if I wanted to show my students how to use the prediction strategy, I would open the guided-practice session with a mini-lesson. Using a picture book, I'd talk through how *I* predict. After the mini-lesson, I invite children to ask questions, to share how they understand and use the strategy, and to voice any confusion they have about it. Then I ask children to work in pairs or small groups to practice the strategy together, using a different picture book. I might also ask them to discuss or write about ways in which the strategy helps them read better. At the end of guided practice, we come together as a class and debrief, sharing what we've learned. We return to the same strategy in the next guided-practice session, until the majority of the class is able to apply it independently. Independent, unconscious application of the reading strategy is the desirable goal.

A Guided-Practice Session Time Line

1. Teacher presents a mini-lesson about the strategy. (7–10 minutes)

2. Students ask questions about the strategy (5–10 minutes)

3. Students break into groups to practice using the strategy with a picture book, a basal selection, or some other reading material that is at their independent reading level. (25–30 minutes)

4. Students write in journals, reflecting on the strategy's benefits. (5 minutes)

5. The class debriefs, sharing what they've discovered. (5–10 minutes)

6. Students who understand the strategy work independently, applying the strategy to a new book in a subsequent guided-practice session, while other students are doing their group work.

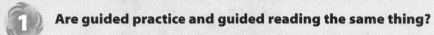

Five Frequently Asked Questions About Guided Practice

1 **Are guided practice and guided reading the same thing?**

One is an extension of the other. Guided practice is a vehicle for the whole class and/or small groups to practice and understand a reading or writing skill, strategy, or technique. It's a way to identify students who don't understand, so you can give them extra support. During guided reading, you and a group of students work on a common problem you identified during guided practice.

2 **How many guided-practice sessions do you devote to a strategy?**

There's no magic number. If you're reviewing a strategy, one to two sessions might be enough. Introduction of new strategies might take 8–10 sessions, including teacher mini-lessons. Let your observations guide your decision about how much time to devote to it.

3 **How do you form groups for guided practice?**

If a strategy is new to students, I introduce it to the whole group. Students who are confused, even after practice sessions, work in small groups with me.

4 **How do you know when a child is ready to try the strategy on his own?**

Observing a child during guided reading and reviewing the student's written work help me evaluate when a child is ready to move on.

5 **What do the kids who "get it" do when you're doing a guided-practice session?**

While I'm working with groups, kids who "get it" work on quiet reading or activities such as SSR, a journal response, or a writing project.

Identifying Students Who Need Conferences

In addition to observing and listening during guided practice, it's essential for you to take notes about students as well. These will inform teaching decisions, such as whether to repeat a mini-lesson, continue practicing a strategy, group students according to their level of understanding, or provide extra practice. You can also use these notes in conferences with students, parents, and administrators.

Using Assessment Checklists

To keep myself—and now you—from being overwhelmed by the note-taking process, I developed checklists that zero in on the specific behaviors I look for (see pages 62–64). Here are some tips for using the checklists, whether you use them during guided practice or at other points in the school day:

☀ Select <u>one</u> issue, such as reading rate, to observe.

☀ Select five to six students, each week, that you'll listen to and observe. If you're new at this, start with one or two students. As you practice and gain confidence in the process, slowly increase the number you observe.

☀ Let students know that you are taking notes, explain why, and tell them you'll share these in a conference.

☀ Jot down brief notes. You can expand upon these during a conference.

☀ Place checklists on a clipboard. Thread a 20-inch piece of rope through the metal clip so you can wear the clipboard like a handbag as you circulate. This helps you keep track of the clipboard as you move from student to student.

Using a Checklist of Reading Strategies

The lists that follow will help you monitor the strategies students use before, while, and after reading. You can note observations and pose questions as you monitor students working in small groups or pairs or when you read students' written work.

Checklist of Strategies Students Use Before Reading

Student's Name _____   **Observation Date** _____

BEFORE-READING STRATEGIES	OBSERVED BEHAVIORS	NOTES
Brainstorm, Cluster, Fast Write, Web, K-W-H-L	Has prior knowledge and experiences.	
Predict	Uses pictures, the title, some of text to support predictions.	
Browse or Skim	Reads captions, boldface headings, words, charts, and graphs to familiarize self with material.	
Question	Uses pictures and title to generate meaningful questions.	
Vocabulary Predictions	Uses knowledge of roots, prefixes, and suffixes to predict meanings. Takes risks. Has broad word knowledge.	

Additional Notes and Questions:

Checklist of Strategies Students Use While Reading

Student's Name _____   **Observation Date** _____

WHILE-READING STRATEGIES	OBSERVED BEHAVIORS	NOTES
Reading Rate	Adjusts rate with purposes, such as skimming, reading to recall, reading for pleasure.	
Predicts & Questions	Confirms and adjusts questions and predictions during reading.	
Self-Corrects	Knows when a word or phrase doesn't make sense and is able to correct without help.	
Monitors Understanding	Can identify parts of a text that are and aren't understood.	
Rereads	Rereads to better recall material, and to revisit favorite parts, and to understand confusing parts.	
Reads/Pauses/Summarizes	Self-monitors reading in science and social studies to check recall.	
Monitors Vocabulary	When stuck on pronouncing and/or understanding a word, uses self-help strategies.	

Additional Notes and Questions:

Checklist of Strategies Students Use After Reading

Student's Name _____ **Observation Date** _____

AFTER-READING STRATEGIES	OBSERVED BEHAVIORS	NOTES
Confirms, Adjusts Predictions	Uses specific examples to adjust predictions.	
Retells	Uses details orally or in writing, to retell a story. Can sequence events.	
Skims & Rereads	Returns to the text to prove points during discussions and for written responses.	
Takes Notes	Can independently note important parts.	
Makes Inferences	Uses dialogue, settings, conflicts, plot, character's decisions and facts to explore implied meanings.	
Reflects on Reading	Draws, talks, and writes about reading.	

Additional Notes and Questions:

READING LOG

Title, Author	Date Completed
Help, Pink Pig C.S. Adler	9-12-94
Welcome to Dead House R.L. Stine	9-16-94
Stay out of the Basement R.L. Stine	9-19-94
The Lion, the Witch, and the Wardrobe C.S. Lewis	9-27-94
Karen's New Year Anne M. Martin	10-4-94
Karen's Carnival Anne M. Martin	10-12-94
Monster Blood R.L. Stine	10-17-94
Say Cheese and Die R.L. Stine	10-20-94
God Must Like Cookies, Too Carol Snyder	10-25-94
Class Clown Johanna Hurwitz	10-28-94
The Teacher's Pet Johanna Hurwitz	11-1-94
Class President Johanna Hurwitz	11-2-94
Once I Was a Plum Tree Johanna Hurwitz	11-11-94
Nora and Mrs. Mind-Your-Own-Business Johanna Hurwitz	11-14-94
The Rabbi's Girls Johanna Hurwitz	11-18-94

Name Sally Stiebel

Checklist of Strategies Students Use While Reading

Name Andy – 6th   Date of Observation 11/12/94

Strategies	Behaviors	Notes
While Reading	**Readers Are Actively Involved With Texts.**	
Reading Rate	Adjusts rate with purposes, such as skimming, reading to recall, reading for pleasure.	
Predicts & Questions	Confirms and adjusts questions and predictions during reading.	
Self-Corrects	Knows when a word or phrase doesn't make sense and is able to correct without help.	
Monitors Understanding	Can identify parts of a text that are and aren't understood.	Andy can do this now—tries strategies to figure out confusing parts.
Rereads	Rereads to better recall material, and to revisit favorite parts, and to understand confusing parts.	We're working on this.
Reads/Pauses/Summarizes	Self-monitors reading in science and social studies to check recall.	
Monitors Vocabulary	When stuck on pronouncing and/or understanding a word, uses self-help strategies.	Andy has guideline sheet and tries to use it—needs 1 to 1 help.

Additional Notes and Questions:

Buddy Andy with a 3rd grader or 2nd grader. Have Andy read his buddy's books & confer with younger child. (Build fluency & self esteem.)

Top: Reading log for a fourth grader.
Above: Checklist for a sixth grader.

Sample Checklist for a Fourth- and Sixth-Grade Student

The completed checklists above illustrate how much information you can collect about students' reading from one survey. After reviewing my notes, I jot down topics and questions to discuss at a conference under "Additional Notes and Questions."

Using the Checklist to Confer With Sally

After reviewing Sally's checklist, which shows smooth sailing with reading, I met briefly with her while making the rounds during her reading-writing workshop. I spent a few minutes celebrating her enthusiasm for reading, the wide range of books her reading log contains, and the notes she takes on author's writing technique and style (See below and page 66).

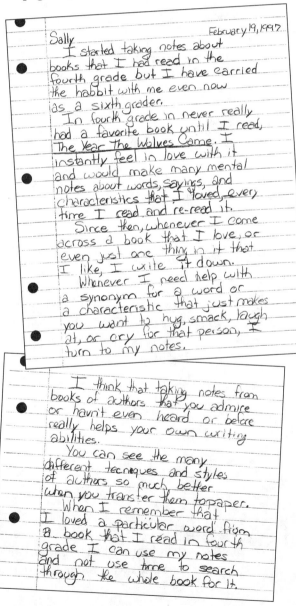

Sally   February 19, 1997

I started taking notes about books that I had read in the fourth grade but I have carried the habbit with me even now as a sixth grader.

In fourth grade in never really had a favorite book until I read, The Year The Wolves Came. I instantly feel in love with it and would make many mental notes about words, sayings, and characteristics that I loved, every time I read and re-read it.

Since then, whenever I come across a book that I love, or even just one thing in it that I like, I write it down.

Whenever I need help with a synonym for a word or a characteristic that just makes you want to hug, smack, laugh at, or cry for that person, I turn to my notes.

I think that taking notes from books of authors that you admire or havn't even heard or before really helps your own writing abilities.

You can see the many different tecniques and styles of authors so much better when you transfer them to paper.

When I remember that I loved a particular word from a book that I read in fourth grade I can use my notes and not use time to search through the whole book for it.

Sally explains her reasons for taking notes while reading.

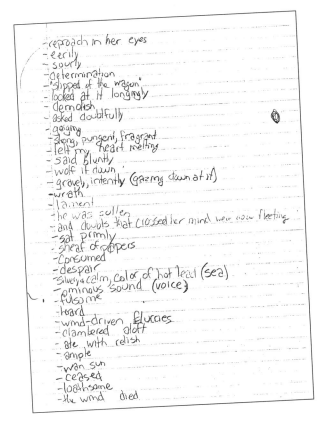

- reproach in her eyes
- eerily
- sourly
- determination
- "slipped off the wagon"
- looked at it longingly
- demolish
- asked doubtfully
- gaging
- strong, pungent, fragrant
- felt my heart melting
- said bluntly
- wolf it down
- gravel, intently (gazing down at it)
- wrath
- lament
- he was sullen
- and doubts that crossed her mind were now fleeting
- sat primly
- sheaf of papers
- consumed
- despair
- silvery & calm, color of hot lead (sea)
- ominous sound (voice)
- fulsome
- hoard
- wind-driven flurries
- clambered aloft
- ate with relish
- ample
- wan sun
- ceased
- loathsome
- the wind died

Sally notes words and phrases from her reading to use in her writing.

Robb: Wow! Your log shows me how much you love to read.

Sally: I read at night but also in the car when mom and I are waiting for Sam [Sally's brother] to finish soccer practice. I'm lucky—I can read in the car on trips—I never get car sick.

Robb: I read on trips, too. It makes the time whiz by. Tell me about the lists of words and phrases you're keeping.

Sally: Every time I read a word or phrase I think is neat, I write it down. When I write and I'm trying to think of a word, I'll read over my lists.

Robb: That's a great strategy, Sally. Would you share it with the class tomorrow? I think other students might try it.

Sally: Sure. [pause] Do you have any Johanna Hurwitz books that I haven't read? I want to read all of hers.

Robb: I'll check and if I find some, I'll bring them tomorrow.

Using the Checklist to Confer With Andy

Andy's checklist indicates that he could benefit from more one-on-one support from me. I schedule a focus conference with him to review some strategies for figuring out the meaning of unknown words and to check on the reading level of books he chooses. After this first meeting, I'll follow up while making the rounds to check on his progress.

TIP BOX

Zero in on One Key Issue

To keep meetings focused, I select one or two topics that I feel are important to each child's development as a reader. I always start with focus conferences and only move into longer meetings with those few students who require 15 or 20 minutes.

Robb: I'm pleased that you are using the guidelines [see page 87] for figuring how to say words with several syllables.

Andy: Yeah—I try, but I still get stuck on them [words].

Robb: I think that part of your struggle has to do with the books you are choosing at this point.

Andy: I know they're hard—but my friends are all reading Robert Westall's books.

Robb: Maybe your mom could read aloud one of Westall's books. But I'd also like you to browse through these books tonight and start one of them. [I give Andy Stone Fox by John Reynolds Gardiner and Alvin Schwartz's More Scary Stories to Tell in the Dark.]

Using Book Discussions and Journal Entries to Tap Topics

It's difficult to monitor five book-discussion groups that are occurring at the same time. Taping each group's discussion makes great demands on my time and has not worked for me. Instead, I have developed several ways of tuning into groups as they talk about books.

Four Manageable Ways to Monitor Book Discussion Groups

1. In a 20–30-minute book discussion period, I observe 2 out of 5 groups. In two weeks, I usually observe each group once. Groups that have difficulty focusing on the task and holding productive discussions receive more of my attention.

2. Four times a year, I fill out a Teacher's Group Evaluation Form (see below) on each group member, focusing on the items listed under *one* heading each time. If necessary, based on my observations, I'll help the group set goals and follow up by sitting in and conferring at their next meeting.

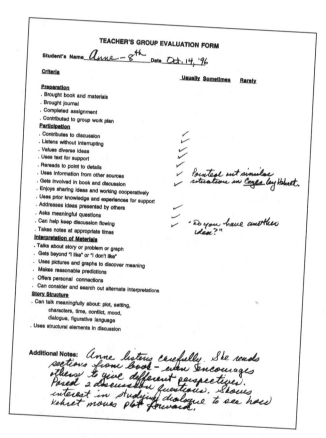

A book discussion evaluation. Notice that you can write comments on the form.

Teacher's Group Evaluation Form

Student's Name _____ **Date** _____

CRITERIA	USUALLY	SOMETIMES	RARELY

Preparation

- Brings book and materials
- Brings journal
- Completes assignment
- Helps group plan agenda

Participation

- Contributes to discussion
- Listens without interrupting
- Values diverse ideas
- Uses text for support
- Rereads to point to details
- Uses prior knowledge and experiences for support
- Addresses ideas presented by others
- Asks meaningful questions
- Can help keep discussion flowing
- Gets involved in book and discussion
- Enjoys sharing ideas and working cooperatively
- Takes notes at appropriate times

Interpretation of Materials

- Talks about story or problem or questions
- Gets beyond "I like it" or "I don't like"
- Uses pictures to explore meaning
- Makes reasonable predictions
- Makes personal connections
- Offers alternate interpretations

Story Structure

- Can talk meaningfully about: plot, setting, characters, time, conflict, mood, dialogue, and figurative language
- Uses structural elements in discussion

Student's Self-Evaluation Form for Group Work

Student's Name _____   **Date** _____

COMMENTS

Preparation

_____ I brought book and materials

_____ I read the appropriate section

_____ I brought journal and pencil

_____ I jotted notes for discussion

Participation (give an example of each checked item)

_____ I made meaningful contributions

_____ I listened to others without interrupting

_____ I asked thoughtful questions

_____ I used book and/or materials to support ideas

_____ I valued the contributions of others

_____ I adjusted my responses when appropriate

Behavior

_____ I abided by guidelines class set

_____ I used my group discussion voice

_____ I supported others

_____ I talked about the task the group agreed on

_____ I helped keep the discussion going

STUDENT'S SELF-EVALUATION FORM FOR GROUP WORK

Student's Name _Jamal – 5th_   Date _11/3/94_

Criteria	Yes	No	Comments

Preparation

. Brought book and materials   ✓
. Read appropriate section   ✓
. Brought journal and pencil   ✓
. Completed all work group agreed upon

Participation

. Made meaningful contributions   *2*   ✓
. Listened to others without interrupting   ✓
. Asked meaningful questions   ✓
. Used book and/or materials to support ideas   ✓
. Valued the contributions of others   ✓
. Modified responses when appropriate   ✓
. Took notes when appropriate

Behavior

. Abided by guidelines class set   ✓
. Used group discussion voice   ✓   _sometimes I get loud._
. Stuck to agenda set by group   ✓   _most of the time_
. Supported other members
. Focused talk on task at hand   ✓
. Helped keep discussion going   _I answer to when Tim asket queston._

Additional Notes:

I'm geting beter. Intrupted 1 time.

Goal: Tak notes

A fifth grader self-evaluates his work in a discussion group.

3. While I observe two groups during a class period, students in the other groups can fill out a Student's Self-Evaluation Form for Group Work (see left)  every four to six weeks. I collect these and write a short comment on each one. Students store these in their reading folders. Any concerns I have can be discussed the next day.

4. Every 2–3 weeks, 10 minutes before class ends, I ask students to summarize their group's book discussions, or explore an issue the class or group raised. These reflections—which students record in their reading journals—help me assess each student's ability to recall a discussion and to use examples to support a position. The summaries of two eighth graders, on the next page, illustrate the varied level of recall of the same discussion.

BOOK STUDENTS DISCUSSED: *California Blue* by David Klass

TOPIC: What did John value? What did Mr. Rodgers, John's dad, value? [discussed after reading 1/3 of the book]

Audrey's Summary

Here's what we talked about: John and his dad like sports. His dad was a football hero and had no respect for John because John ran track. They didn't get along.

After reading Audrey's summary, I set up a focus conference. My goal was to provide Audrey with a strategy to improve her summaries. Here is a transcription of the conference:

Robb: Tell me how you go about writing your discussion summary.

Audrey: I just write what I remember. [long pause during which she rereads summary] But I guess I'm not remembering enough.

Robb: How can you help yourself remember more?

Audrey: William and the others take notes. But that's hard for me.

Robb: What makes taking notes hard?

Audrey: I try to write everything and then get lost and forget.

Robb: That is hard. It's easier to write down key phrases or words.

Audrey: I think I'd still get behind.

Robb: You could ask the speaker to repeat his idea.

Audrey: That's hard, too. They'll think I'm dumb.

Robb: I understand how you feel. Can we agree that you'll try jotting down some key words and phrases after the next book discussion?

Audrey: I'll try.

Two days later, Audrey tried this strategy and found that she was able to write much more. Now she was willing to continue to practice this strategy, and, over time, I expected her to progress even more.

The student who wrote the second summary did a terrific job. William deserved to hear me praise his efforts. While making the rounds, I paused and said, "Your summary really gave me insights into the group's discussion and process—it was outstanding." Then I wrote comments on a sticky note that William placed under his journal entry.

William's Summary

Our group first talked about what John valued, then we discussed the things that his dad valued. John loved to run and was on the track team. He had a passion for nature, loved his biology class and teacher, and even subscribed to a nature magazine. Mr. Rodger's favorite sport was football, and he was a football hero during high school. He has never gone to a track meet of John's, using the fact that he works when John runs as an excuse. Mr. Rodgers does not understand or appreciate John's interest in nature and biology and made his son stop the subscription to the nature magazine. Right now, Mr. Rodgers values living, as he has found out that he has Leukemia and has a 30% chance of making it. At the end, we wondered if Mr. Rodger's illness and John's guilt for hating his father would cause a huge conflict in the story.

Sticky-Note Comments

- detailed examples from book

- included several things each valued

- topic sentence told focus up front

- Group set a purpose for reading-on when I wondered about a conflict between John and his dad.

Some Open-Ended Questions to Move Book Discussions Along

☀ Can you find an example from the story that supports your idea?

☀ Are there additional pieces of support?

☀ Does anyone have another point of view?

☀ Are there different responses to the passage that was just read and discussed?

☀ Does that comment raise questions?

Responses That Value Diverse Ideas

☀ I appreciate your willingness to share a totally different point of view. Your evidence certainly supports that idea.

☀ You disagreed but honored your classmate's idea.

☀ Sounds like an interesting position. Can you find evidence to support it?

TIP BOX

Ways to Raise the Level of Discussions

I teach the art of effective book discussions by placing a small group onstage in front of the class. This gives me a chance to demonstrate how to ask questions, keep a discussion going, value diverse points of view, and use examples from the material as support. Usually all groups ask to go on center stage. Once I've presented the model, I invite students to create book discussion guidelines. Periodically, I review rules with the class to refresh students' minds.

Finding Conference Topics by Observing Students' Independent Reading

Watching your students read silently can be a rich source of conference topics. Some students settle down immediately and read the entire time. Sure, they might pause and show a friend a "great part," but they have the ability to concentrate for 30 minutes and select books that interest them.

There are students who seem to take forever to settle down and read. They need to drink water, visit the rest room, try a chair or beanbag or find a spot under the table, stretch, and stare into space.

The checklist on page 75 helps you monitor behaviors during sustained silent reading and evaluate students' written work on independent reading. Once each marking period, I complete a checklist on each child, then add notes during a focus conference. Here are the checklists of a reluctant reader in the seventh grade and a fourth grader who loves to read.

A Checklist For Monitoring Independent Reading

Name _David — 7th_   Date _9/6/95 – 11/6/95_

Observations   Teacher's Notes

Book Log Entries

Number of Books   _2_

Variety of Titles   _both are mysteries_

Sustained Silent Reading

Selects books on independent level   _usually picks books that are too hard_

Gets started quickly   _takes 10-15 min. to settle into reading_

Self-helps before seeking peer or teacher assistance   _doesn't seek help_

Shows pleasure in reading through journal entries, talk, and projects   _openly says, "I hate to read."_

Written Work

Book reviews   —

Critical paragraphs, essays   —

Projects   _likes to draw pictures_

Dialogue Journals

Oral Work

Book talks   —

Reading fluency   _haltingly_

Oral reading error patterns   _lots of errors in books David picks — too hard for him._

Additional Notes and Questions

Work on getting David to select books he can read with ease. Schedule several 1-to-1 focus conference.

A Checklist For Monitoring Independent Reading

Name _Samantha — 4th_   Date _1/6/97 – 2/24/97_

Observations   Teacher's Notes

Book Log Entries

Number of Books   _7_

Variety of Titles   _mystery, realistic fiction, books on bats_

Sustained Silent Reading

Selects books on independent level   _uses 5 finger regularly_

Gets started quickly   _always_   _goes with partner to the library_

Self-helps before seeking peer or teacher assistance   _can usually work issues out alone_

Shows pleasure in reading through journal entries, talk, and projects   _yes!_

Written Work

Book reviews   —

Critical paragraphs, essays   —

Projects   _makes clay figures of characters_

Dialogue Journals   —   _loves to do dress-up reports_

Oral Work

Book talks   _enjoys "advertising" her favorite titles to others_

Reading fluency   _yes!_

Oral reading error patterns

Additional Notes and Questions   _Try to introduce Sam to historical fiction — suggest Sign of the Beaver The Salem Faced West_

Finding Conference Topics in Students' Self-Evaluations

"Too many of my fifth graders don't settle down and read, so why should I schedule silent reading?" a frustrated teacher asked me when I helped in her classroom for a few days. As we talked about this issue, the teacher admitted that out of 28 children, she had 5–6 students who read little or nothing during 30-minute periods. Most of the class, however, used and treasured this time.

So often we focus on the behavior of a few students, and they dominate our evaluation of a classroom practice. Rather than eliminate a program that most students rated top-notch, I suggested that she open and close reading sessions with a self-evaluation sheet (see page 78, top). Now students had to decide on the amount of reading they planned to complete, note what they had accomplished, and compare their goal with the outcome.

These sheets contained information that enabled the teacher to change some behaviors as well as applaud students' progress as she made the rounds.

It's easy to scan these sheets and address students who require support at the outset of SSR. You can then briefly visit with others, giving them positive feedback and encouragement to continue the terrific work.

TIP BOX

Reading Contracts

After the first month of school, when I've learned a great deal about my students' reading lives, I introduce independent-reading contracts. Each month, students set a goal, in writing, in which they commit to reading a specific number of books. Some students read three to four books a month; others might read one title. Students learn to pace themselves and can see growth as the year unfolds. During the month, they record titles in their reading logs and then use them for book talks and reviews, projects, and analytical paragraphs.

A Checklist For Monitoring Independent Reading

Name _____ **Date** _____

Book Log Entries

Number of Books

Variety of Titles

Sustained Silent Reading

Selects books on independent level

Gets started quickly

Self-helps before seeking
peer or teacher assistance

Shows pleasure in reading through
journal entries, talk, and projects

Written Work

Book reviews

Critical paragraphs, essays

Projects

Dialogue Journals

Oral Work

Book talks

Reading fluency

Oral reading error patterns

Additional Notes and Questions

Conferring With Adam

I often open a conference with the students' words. I handed Adam, a fifth grader, his self-evaluation and read, "I planned to read two chapters today, but I don't like the book and I don't know if I can change it. So I drew pictures in my journal. My goal for next SSR is to read two chapters." Here is a transcription of our exchange:

Adam: Yeah, I've read 3 chapters and don't like it. I like funny books.

Robb: Do you want to change books?

Adam: Sure. But I don't know if I can change it. It's due in a week.

Robb: Ask your teacher and maybe she'll give you an extension if you need one. You might find a book that you'll finish quickly. [Adam learned an important lesson about communicating his feelings and needs to his teacher. This conversation might never have taken place if Adam had not filled out a self-evaluation.]

Adam's teacher not only agreed to a change, but she suggested he read *Class Clown* by Johanna Hurwitz—a book Adam adored. Students' self-evaluative comments provide great openers because they usually contain honest explanations. The student examples that follow contain the seeds for effecting positive change and growth in a brief conference.

※ I didn't read today because I'm hungry and all I could think of was food. (Grade 4)

※ I read one page because I don't understand this book. I can't say a lot of the words. (Grade 6)

※ I didn't read my book today because I left it at home and didn't want to say this because I've done this all week. (Grade 5)

※ I didn't choose this book. My dad says I have to read it because he loved it. Well I don't like it and want to choose my own. (Grade 7)

T I P   B O X

Using a Workshop Self-Evaluation Form and a Reading Strategy Conference Form

Use the Workshop Self-evaluation form once or twice a week when you are trying to change students' patterns. Once students are managing their time well, ask them to self-evaluate once or twice a month. Self-evaluations that invite students to write about a reading strategy or how they have improved their reading offer insights into students' thinking and understanding that you can discuss at conferences. Students can work in pairs or independently to evaluate how they apply a strategy using the Reading Strategy Conference form (see page 78, bottom).

Reading Strategy Conference

This conference was held on April 2, 1997 between:

Name Sally

Name Reilly

Write the strategy you practiced and discussed:
Taking notes in different ways, science, history, special words and phrases from books.

How did the strategy help you?
Notes I take help the reading stick in my mind. It helps me to study.

What did you learn from your partner?
That Reilly takes notes from listening by finding key phrases and words.

What other strategies did you use along with the one you practiced?
I skim and reread the pages in the book before I take notes.

Sally and Reilly have a conference on note-taking strategies.

Reading Strategy Conference

This conference was held on April 2, 1997 between:

Name Reilly

Name Sally

Write the strategy you practiced and discussed:
Taking notes in history, science, English, and math from what the teacher says and from the book sometimes.

How did the strategy help you?
When ever I take notes it's easier for me to remember what we learned about and it's easier than just looking through the book again

What did you learn from your partner?
Sally copies special words and phrases from a book that she likes

What other strategies did you use along with the one you practiced?
Taking notes from listening/choosing key phrases and words

From the book/I skim and reread the most important parts then take notes.

Paired and Solo Self-Evaluations

Sixth graders Sally and Reilly confer with one another on note-taking strategies (see above, left and right). Though they use different strategies, both find that what they do helps them in history and science. Paired evaluations permit students to learn from one another and can also be discussed at individual and group conferences.

Fourth graders write about visualizing new vocabulary in strategy notebooks. They point out that drawing reflects their level of understanding. The selections that follow illustrate the range of responses in one class and how easy it is to identify students who need a conference:

❉ When I draw a word like eruption, the picture helps me see it and hear the sounds. I see a volcano with red lava pouring out and animals and people running away. I hear the roar of the explosion and animals and people crying and being scared. It's amazing how pictures of words can make me see so much.

❉ Drawing pictures doesn't help because I don't see pictures of words in my head.

❉ I make pictures of words and of characters and places when I read. The pictures help me know what's happening and what words mean.

Continued on page 79

Workshop Self-Evaluation

Name _____ **Date** _____

- ☀ I plan to accomplish the following in today's workshop:

- ☀ What did I accomplish?

- ☀ How can I use my work time to accomplish more?

- ☀ Here are my goal(s) for next workshop class:

Reading & Writing Conferences Scholastic Professional Books, 1998

Reading Strategy Conference

This conference was held on _____ **between:**

Name _____

Name _____

- ☀ Write the strategy you practiced and discussed:

- ☀ How did the strategy help you?

- ☀ What did you learn from your partner?

- ☀ What other strategies did you use along with the one you practiced?

Reading & Writing Conferences Scholastic Professional Books, 1998

✴ I do this without drawing and like it better when it's in my head.

✴ If I picture a word, then I understand it and remember it forever.

Some Ideas to Think About

Here are seven statements that focus my attention on what students can do. I reread the list frequently because it reminds me to listen to and communicate with students and to offer opportunities for them to reflect, self-evaluate, and set goals.

My goal is to identify students' strong points and explore ways to use their strengths to overcome difficulties. The more information I collect, the better equipped I am to make informed teaching decisions and adjust classroom instruction.

REFLECT ON THESE READING ASSESSMENT STATEMENTS

1. I focus on what each child knows and can do.

2. I discover what the child can do independently.

3. I observe the child working in a group.

4. I communicate my observations to the students.

5. I include the students when setting goals and planning interventions.

6. I invite students to self-evaluate and use these evaluations to support them.

7. I record some of my observations and use them in my progress reports to parents and administrators.

CHAPTER 5

Conferences That Monitor and Improve Reading

very time a teacher tells me that a student isn't working because he's lazy or doesn't care about school, neon lights flash inside my head. "What makes you say that?" I gently ask. Usually, a list of unproductive behaviors pours out—for example, doesn't listen, talks when everyone is working, hasn't turned in homework for several days, doesn't participate in group discussions, doesn't care if he loses recesses.

Next, I ask the teacher, "Have you conferred with the student, shared your observations, and asked why these things are happening?" Most students have a pretty good idea why their learning patterns have changed or why they appear uninvolved in their work. The responses that follow illustrate a variety of factors that might cause a student to shut down at school. Very rarely do such behaviors result from laziness.

※ I don't remember anything I read in the book we're using. The others all seem to remember and talk in groups and write. Even when I reread, I don't remember a lot. (Grade 8)

※ We just found out that my granddad has cancer, and all I can think about is how sick he is. (Grade 6)

※ I hate the book we all have to read. It's boring and it doesn't make any sense, so I don't read it. (Grade 5)

※ It takes me forever to read. I have trouble saying lots of words. I don't finish it [reading] at school or at night. I keep getting it for not doing my work. (Grade 4)

When students' behavior patterns are negative or unproductive, wait to draw conclusions until you've asked them why. After conferring with these students, the teachers discovered that the books were too difficult for the students in grades eight and five. It turned out that the fourth grader struggled so much with decoding that reading was slow and ponderous. Once the problem has been identified, then teachers can search for strategies that support students and enable them to experience success. In a reading conference, teachers can explore and discover reasons why students behave in disruptive and unproductive ways. In addition, reading conferences perform these important functions:

※ Monitor students' application of reading strategies.

※ Evaluate students' patterns of error or miscues.

※ Discuss books students read at school and at home.

※ Evaluate students' written responses to their reading.

※ Evaluate the variety of books students select.

Longer Individual Conferences

Five- to ten-minute focus conferences zero in on an issue that the teacher or student raises. But there are times when longer conferences are in order, and these are the ones that pose scheduling difficulties. The two that follow are well worth the time.

Getting-to-Know-You Conferences

PURPOSE: To get to know my students, to discuss their reading and writing experiences and attitudes, and to get a handle on the skills and strategies they've acquired.

CONTENT: We discuss their responses to the Seven Questions About Reading (see page 53), the Reading Survey (see page 52), and the Information Sheets completed by parents (see page 16).

SCHEDULING: I schedule two conferences a day and can meet with thirty children in three weeks.

Conferences That Support Students' Reading and Writing

PURPOSE: To support readers and writers who require extra time to understand how to use and apply reading and writing skills and strategies.

CONTENT: Students and I work on issues such as revision, editing, reading comprehension, note-taking, summarizing, and figuring out the meanings of unknown words.

SCHEDULING: I schedule these conferences throughout the year as needed. Sometimes I ask students to meet me at lunch recess or before school if they arrive on an early bus. Most of the time I meet with students when the rest of the class works independently.

TIP BOX

How To's of Reading Folders

Build a student's reading folder over the entire school year. Use a plain manila file folder. Store these in a plastic crate or in your filing cabinet. Place copies of read-aloud records, teacher-observation notes, and single items—such as the Reading Survey or responses to the Seven Questions—into folders as soon as each is completed. Add other important items, such as photocopied journal entries and conference notes. As folders move up with students, reduce the number of last year's items, and select two pieces that reflect the reader's strengths.

Making Use of Reading Folders During Conferences

If I'm lucky, at the start of the year I also receive a reading folder for each child to use at getting-to-know-you conferences.

A reading folder is not a portfolio, though some of the pieces in a reading folder might also be in a student's portfolio. It is a folder compiled by the teacher to document a child's reading journey from the beginning to the end of the year. Selections include samples from work, such as students' journal entries or read-aloud records, throughout the year.

Reading folders include valuable information that can be discussed with students, parents, other teachers, and administrators. A folder's contents also support a teacher's interventions and instructional decisions.

For each item you've selected to place in the reading folder, photocopy a sample from the beginning and end of the year. If there is a shortage of samples from any one category, attach a note briefly explaining why. For example, if a child is reading well above grade level, then place in the folder a note with that information.

Some Suggestions for What to Include in a Reading Folder

- Read-Aloud Checklist
- Reading Log
- Journal entries
- Reading Survey
- Parent Information Sheet
- Book Conference notes
- Teacher-Observation notes
- Retellings and/or Summaries

How to Use Getting-to-Know-You Conferences

After reviewing the data I have collected on each child, I map out a schedule and first meet with students who have one or several of the following characteristics:

- There are many unanswered questions on the Reading Survey.

- The parents have expressed concerns over the child's reading.

- Students frankly write that they "hate to read," find reading "boring," or admit that they are "weak readers."

- Last year's reading folder indicates that this student lacks strategies, such as pronouncing multisyllable words and figuring out the meaning of unknown words.

- All standardized testing and information from last year's teacher indicates that the child reads below grade level.

Schedule students who are proficient readers later, but make sure that they receive feedback as soon as you've read their surveys. These children need and deserve attention and recognition too. On a sticky note, write comments that honor their reading strengths and tastes.

Each student brings a free-choice reading book to the conference. Students choose books by using the five-finger method, selecting titles they can comfortably read.

Getting-to-Know-You Conferences

I open the conference with all the positive things I noticed on the Reading Survey and Parent Information Sheet. We talk about hobbies, favorite sports, movies, books, music. My goal is to listen to the child talk. Toward the end of our meeting, I invite the student to open the book and read one to two pages aloud. We sit side-by-side as the child reads so I can follow along in the text. I check off items on the Read-Aloud Checklist that are fine and jot as many notes as I can next to items that I need to reflect upon (see below).

Read Aloud Checklist

Student's Name _Keith - 5th Grade_   Date _9/24/96_

Title and Author _The Half-a-Moon Inn by Paul Fleischman_   Read pages _14-16_

Observations   Notes and Examples

Reads fluently with expression and in meaningful chunks.
Phrases reading within punctuation marks.

· parts read in chunks - when a word stumped Keith - he'd stop & go to word-to-word reading
· after Keith tries to say a "hard word" he races through commas & periods as he reads on

Reads word to word.

Sometimes

Reads through punctuation.
Note how many times this occurred.

Frequently hesitates before words.
Write words, page, and paragraph.

page 15, "mired" #2
"stranded & Crafts bury,"
page 16, "glancing nervously," top of page

Struggles pronouncing multi-syllable words.
List the words.

mired, shivering, Crafts bury, burlap, glancing

Repeats words and phrases many times.
Note words and phrases that were repeated.

At dawn he; but nowhere was he become mired in; He packed his; stranded

Needs frequent prompting on words.
List the words you helped student pronounce.

prompted 3 times - "mired, Craftsbury; glancing"

Makes word substitutions.
Write the text word and above it write the substituted word.

warmed	stuck	attached
warned	stranded	attacked
brillo		
burlap		

Omits words.
List omitted words and the word that comes after each omitted word.

Retelling and comprehension.
Rich details told in sequence. Connects selection to the entire story.

Keith, despite his errors, understood what the story was about. He explained the significance of the Inn, how Aaron got there, etc.

Teachers Comments, Questions, and Recommendations:

Keith admitted that he struggled through the book, but his older brother told him it was a great story. When Keith read from a book that was near his comfort level (Pirate's Promise by Clyde Bulla) he read fluently.

Keith agreed to use the 5 finger method. Later in the day, I gave him 6 titles to keep on his desk. Try these, I suggested, and read those you enjoy — put back any that don't catch your interest.

Schedule an analytical reading inventory.

Read-Aloud Checklists help you identify reading difficulties.

Read-Aloud Checklist

Student's Name _____   **Date** _____

Title and Author _____   **Read pages** _____

OBSERVATIONS	NOTES AND EXAMPLES
Reads fluently with expression and in meaningful chunks. *Phrases reading within punctuation marks.*	
Reads word to word.	
Reads through punctuation. *[Note how many times this occurred.]*	
Frequently hesitates before words. *[Write words, page, and paragraph.]*	
Struggles pronouncing multisyllable words. *[List the words.]*	
Repeats words and phrases many times. *[Note words and phrases that were repeated.]*	
Needs frequent prompting on words. *[List the words you helped student pronounce.]*	
Makes word substitutions. *[Write the text word above it; write the substituted word.]*	
Omits words. *[List omitted words and the word that comes after each omitted word.]*	
Retelling and comprehension. Rich details told in sequence. Connects selection to the entire story.	

Teachers Comments, Questions, and Recommendations:

Using the Checklist to Figure Out Who Needs a Longer Conference

The data collected from this checklist enables you to distinguish those students who require several 15-minute follow-up conferences from those you can support in making-the-rounds, spotlighting, or focus conferences.

The checklist is not meant to be a substitute for administering the Analytical Reading Inventory, developed by Mary Lynn Woods and Alden J. Moe, or the Formal Miscue Analysis, developed by Yetta Goodman. Instead, it provides insights that can help you consider these questions:

- Does the child need several follow-up conferences?

- Should the teacher or a reading specialist administer an Analytical Reading Inventory or a Formal Miscue Analysis?

- Should the child be referred to a reading specialist?

- Would this student benefit from the support of a reading buddy?

- What kind of support can I ask the family to provide?

- How can I accommodate the curriculum so this child will experience success and make progress?

- Can I organize and confer with a group of students wrestling with the same reading problem?

Know When to Get Extra Help

New teachers who have a large number of struggling readers should seek the help of a reading resource teacher or an experienced colleague in analyzing students' oral reading errors.

Sometimes experienced teachers feel overwhelmed when they have a large number of students who need monitoring and support. A supervisor, librarian, or parent can help with follow-up conferences.

Small-Group Conferences for Struggling Readers

Quite often, struggling readers wrestle with similar problems—for example, they have difficulty pronouncing long, multi-syllable words or figuring out the meaning of new words. Holding a group conference not only saves you time but also lets each student know that he or she is not the only one struggling. Moreover, participants learn to support themselves and one another.

Providing students with a series of steps to follow can assist them in pronouncing and figuring out the meaning of unfamiliar words. Model the process with students, and then have them work in pairs or groups. Give students a copy of the guidelines that follow so they can refer to these when solving problems on their own.

Strategies to Use When You're Stuck on a Hard Word

☀ Instead of guessing, reread the sentence containing the word you don't know and the sentences that come before and after it.

☀ Try to find clues in those sentences to help you figure out the word.

If that doesn't work...

☀ Look closely at the word.

☀ If the word has a prefix, try to say it— then take it off.

☀ If the word has a suffix, try to say it— then take it off.

☀ Look at the base or root word that's left. Does it resemble another word you know? For example, the base felon resembles and melon. Try saying the base word, then blend all the word parts together.

☀ Reread the sentence and see if the word makes sense.

If that doesn't work...

☀ Ask a classmate or adult for help.

☀ Look up the word in the dictionary.

Strategies That Help You Figure Out What a Word Means

When an unknown word makes a sentence or paragraph confusing, and you can't continue to read, try these suggestions:

Be a Word Detective and Look for Clues in...

☀ other words or phrases in the sentence. If or, is, or such as follows the difficult word, look for a synonym or similar word close by.

☀ the illustrations, diagrams, photographs, and charts.

☀ the sentences that came before and after the sentence with the unknown word.

Pull Out the Clues and...

☀ look for familiar words and phrases.

☀ think of a synonym.

☀ reread the sentence with the unfamiliar word to make sure you understand its meaning.

If that doesn't work,

☀ ask a classmate for help.

☀ ask an adult for help.

Conferences on Students' Free-Choice Reading

When students complete several books each month, it's impossible to discuss every title with them in a conference. Trust must exist between teacher and student that their monthly reading contracts have been completed. Sure, some students will list books in their reading logs that they haven't read. My hope is that as the year progresses, these students will fulfill their reading contracts because the books are at their comfort level and they've begun to enjoy reading fluently. (See page 74 for Reading Contract Tip Box.)

The Autumn One-on-One Book Conference

In October, I invite students to select a book they'd like to discuss in a conference with me. Students also have the option to request a conference earlier in the month. Since these take four to five minutes, it's easy to meet with every student in one week. Students must bring their book to the conference. On a Book Conference Form, I record the conference highlights (see upper right). Sometimes I need to ask additional questions, which I call probes, to help the child respond. I've included examples of these in italics on the conference form on page 89.

Book Conference Form

Date _Nov. 20, 1996_
Name _Tyler - Grade 8_   Name _Mrs. Robb_
Preparation Check: ✓ brought book   ✓ brought pencil
Title and Author _I Am The Cheese by Robert Cormier_

Why did you choose the book? My older brother read it two years ago. When I saw it on the book shelf, I remembered he really liked it.

What did you like? I liked the flashbacks—I could put things together that way. It was sad, but could really happen.

Can you connect the title to the story? "The cheese stands alone"—the end of the game in the "Farmer in the Dell." He's the last person alive in his family. 1st and last paragraph in book are the same—it's like he's starting over. The main character is the cheese. His dad died and he's alone. It's about father's and sons. The son will never be able
How did the reading go?

Suggestions for next book. Tyler wants to read another Cormier book. I suggested, After the First Death. I also suggested he look into Will Hobbs & Mark Talbert.

Title continued: to tell his dad all the things in his heart. His dad's dead, but the memories will help.

Teacher–student book conferences honor readers and reading.

Book Conference Form

Student's Name _____ **Date** _____

Brought Book _____

Title and Author _____

☀ ## Why did you choose the book?

Is it a topic you love?
Did someone help you find the book?

☀ ## What did you like about the story, a character, the setting?

Can you find a favorite part, read it, and explain why you liked it?
Did you have a lot in common with a character? Explain what it was.
Did the author create suspense or make you laugh? Can you find a suspenseful or funny passage and read it?

☀ ## Can you connect the title to the story?

What about the character was reflected in the title?
Were the words in the title used in the story? In what part? Why?
Did the title point to a certain character or event? Explain.

☀ ## How did the reading go?

Did you enjoy the book? Why?
Did you read with ease?
Were there any parts that confused you?
Was it difficult to stop reading once you got into it?
Did you learn any new words?

☀ ## Suggestions for next book:

The Rationale of the Book-Conference Form

Asking "What did you like?" offers students an opportunity to talk about a favorite character, setting, passage, or illustration. "Can you connect the title to the story?" invites students to draw conclusions about the story as they link plot and conflicts to the title. The reason for asking "How did the reading go?" is to emphasize that reading books ought to be enjoyable. If it's not, adjustments need to be made so that students find books at their independent reading level. Under "Suggestions for next book," I list a few titles and point out that while the child is free to select other books, he or she might enjoy these.

When conferences are completed, I compile a list of titles rated "top-notch" by students. I write them on the chalkboard and suggest that others in the class might want to read these. I also point out some of the ways students chose books, so they realize that friends, family members, teachers, and librarians can make terrific suggestions.

Partner Book-Conferences on Free-Choice Reading

After the first round of book conferences, I have pairs of students confer about free-choice reading selections. Then students and I alternate so that I hold book conferences every other month. Take the time to demonstrate these easy steps so that students will understand the process:

Mini-Lesson Guidelines for Demonstrating Partner Book-Conferences

[Teacher models with a student.]

1. Model with a book or story that all students have read.

2. Select a topic to discuss with your partner from two to three topics on the blackboard.

3. Show how you record notes. Include your name, the book's title, the topic you've selected, and examples from the book you plan to discuss.

4. Discuss your book, using the notes to guide your comments.

5. Encourage students to raise questions about your discussions and about the process.

6. Tell who you would recommend the book to and offer reasons.

7. Explain that students must bring their free-reading book to class in order to prepare for partner conferences.

An entire class can complete partner book-conferences in one 45-minute period. Students can find and sit in comfortable places around the classroom or side-by-side at their desks.

Using the steps that follow, guide students through the process until they can independently confer in pairs.

Classroom Management Tips for Partner Book-Conferences

PART I: PREPARATION AND LISTENING:

1. Allow about 15 minutes for students to choose a topic, think about it, and take notes. Encourage them to skim their books and find examples that support their topic.

2. Use the remaining 30 minutes to get partner conferences going.

3. Organize the class into partners.

4. Help students complete the Partner Conference Form.

5. Listen first. Each partner has 10 minutes to discuss his or her book, raise questions, and talk about whether he or she would recommend the book to others.

PART II: WRITING:

6. Have students use the last 10 minutes to fill in the Partner Book-Conference Record Sheet.

7. Turn notes in with the conference form.

8. Partners staple or clip notes and conference forms together.

Puss In Boots

Alanna   April 17, 1997

Topic: To pick out a picture and/or a passage and explain why you chose it

Passage: When he'd caught his breath, Puss said: "I hear you can turn yourself into small animals, too, a rat or a mouse for instance. That seems impossible." "It seems impossible, does it?" said the Ogre. A second later the Ogre was gone and a mouse was scurrying across the floor. Puss pounced and caught him and gobbled him up.

Because Puss said that is impossible he egged the Ogre on to get him to turn into a mouse so Puss could eat him.

Allana's notes for her book conference.

The Boy Who Swallowed Snakes

Nick   April 17, 1997

Topic: to explain the authors purpose

I think the authors purpose is do not be greedy or your greediness will take your away of your life away

In the story a man made silver by eating a snake and he thought if he ate more snakes he would be rich. He ate another snake and got a stomach ache

Nick's notes for his book conference.

Partner Book Conference Record Sheet

Student's Name Nick   Grade 5
Partner's Name Alanna   Date 4/17/97
Title and Author of Partner's Book Puss in Boots by C. Perrault
Preparation Checklist: Came with ✓ book ✓ pencil

Tell the topic your partner talked about.
To pick out a picture and or a passage and explain why you chose it

List 2 points your partner discussed.
• when the ogre bragged he could turn into a small rat Puss egged the ogre on so he cold eat him
• Puss couldn't eat a giant ogre but he could eat a mouse

Did your partner recommend the book to you? Explain why or why not.
Alanna recommds the book to boys and gils if you like cats.

Alanna records Nick's discussion of his book.

Partner Book Conference Record Sheet

Student's Name Alanna   Grade 5
Partner's Name Nick   Date 4-17-97
Title and Author of Partner's Book The Boy Who Swallowed Snakes by L. Yep
Preparation Checklist: Came with ✓ book ✓ pencil

Tell the topic your partner talked about. To explain authors purpose

List 2 points your partner discussed.
• don't be greedy or sreediness can take your life away or just make you sick
• the man made silver by eating a snaked he thought if he ate lots of snakes he would get rich — Mr. Ow yang thought if he ate lots of snakes he'd be richer than the emperor

Did your partner recommend the book to you? Explain why or why not.
when he ate the snake he got very sick and he died.
Nick recommends it because little Chow was poor and very kind, and he was able to use his own courage, Both boys and girls would like this story

Nick records Alanna's discussion of his book.

Partner Book-Conference Record Sheet

Student's Name _____

Partner's Name _____ **Date** _____

Title and Author of Partner's Book _____

Preparation Checklist: **Came with:** **book** _____ **pencil** _____

* What topic did your partner discuss?

* List two points your partner discussed.

* Did your partner recommend the book to you? Explain why or why not.

Partner Book Conference Record Sheet

Student's Name _Missy Bryant_ Grade 8

Partner's Name _Margaret Harris_ Date _Apr. 21, 1997_

Title and Author of Partner's Book _Prairie Songs, Pam Conrad_

Preparation Checklist: Came with _✓_ book _____ pencil

Tell the topic your partner talked about.

Margaret talked about the authors purpose and theme for writing the book.

List 2 points your partner discussed.

1. She liked how the character gave information about her life.

2. She liked how the story gave an example of people who encountered problems on the Prairies.

Did your partner recommend the book to you? Explain why or why not.

No, the reading was slow. The exciting parts didn't last long. But if you like boring stuff + a different life, read it!

• Notes •

A Touch of Chill, by Joan Aiken
Missy April 21, 1997

1. The character or situation you connected to and why.

Short → "The cat flap and the apple pie"
Story
NOTES - George Crask + his mother were busy cleaning for company.
- @ the last minute people called to come to lunch.
@ the time George was busy putting in a cat flap for his cat.
- everyone was running around + the cats were chasing each other. Then the company called and said they weren't coming. So George ran outside + said "I'm fed up, I'm going to turn into a tree."
- Sometimes I feel like that. Everything gets hectic + all I want to do is turn into someone else or something else.

Missy's conference with Margaret (top).
An eighth grader's notes for her book conference (above).

After I skim through their conference notes, I place them in a plastic tray so students can read them during workshop. (Return an old batch to students before placing new ones in the tray.) By reading one another's notes, students learn how to improve their own, and they discover new books to read. Not every student chooses to read conference forms, and that's okay.

As you read through partner conferences, note the names of students who did not come prepared and whose recorded notes were too general. For example, a fourth grader conferring about *Cam Jansen and the Triceratops Pops Mystery* by David Adler (Viking) chose "mystery genre" as her topic. The child's examples, "clues and a detective," could have been for any book and were not specific enough to convince me that the book had been read. In a case like this, I confer with the student in a follow-up focus conference and try to collect story-specific examples. If the child hasn't read the book, then we negotiate a way to complete the work.

Suggested Topics for Partner Book-Conferences

Have partners discuss topics that you have already modeled, practiced, and used in class.

On large chart paper, post items from the list that follows. Choose those you believe are most appropriate for your students.

Prior to partner book-conferences, I write two to three topics on the blackboard and invite students to select the one that they want to discuss. Once students are ready to confer without my guidance, they can select a topic from the chart.

SOME TOPICS FOR PARTNER BOOK-CONFERENCES

☀ Retell a chapter or favorite part.

☀ Discuss changes in the main character from beginning to end of story.

☀ State a major problem a character faced and how it was resolved.

☀ Focus on one key conflict in the story and the outcome.

☀ Discuss the character and/or situation you personally connected to, and why

☀ Identify the genre and give three to four examples from the story that illustrate the genre's structure.

☀ Discuss new information you learned.

☀ Select a favorite illustration or passage from the story, and explain why you chose it.

☀ Describe two settings and explain how each affected the plot or action or a character's decisions.

☀ Discuss the author's purpose or the theme of the book.

☀ Explain how the title connects to the story.

☀ Discuss two events that greatly influenced the main character.

☀ Select and read a short passage in the book that really spoke to you. Connect the passage to your experiences and to the story.

☀ Predict/Support/Confirm or Adjust

Tip Box

Sticky-Note Strategy

Set up a way to respond to the prediction strategy before students read their books. Give each child two sticky notes. Have them write "Predict and Support" at the top and "Confirm or Adjust" near the bottom. Then have them place a sticky note at the end of the second or third chapter and another at the end of the next-to-the-last chapter. Students can jot down notes on these and use them during book conferences.

Some Ideas to Think About

*T*eacher-student book conferences enable you to monitor students' reading and to nudge students to reflect deeply on their books through questions and probes. As soon as possible, involve students in conferring with one another about books. Once they are comfortable with the process, many will ask to confer more often.

Getting students to think deeply about their books can occur during the types of reading experiences you offer students in grades 4 through 8. A balanced reading workshop contains teacher-led, student-led, and independent activities. Reflect on the kinds of reading listed below, and think about how you integrate each one into your program:

A BALANCED READING WORKSHOP INCLUDES THESE 7 ELEMENTS:

1. DAILY READ-ALOUDS *(teacher-led)*
   Teacher develops interest in reading, introduces students to different genres, and expands students knowledge of language.

2. GUIDED PRACTICE OF READING STRATEGIES *(teacher-led)*
   Teacher introduces strategies and provides opportunities for students to practice and

discuss them. There is a great deal of conversation among students about each strategy.

3. GUIDED READING IN SMALL GROUPS *(teacher-led)*
   Teacher supports small groups as students discuss the meaning of a story. Students learn to respond to texts, practice reading strategies, and learn to make inferences and solve problems, such as figuring out the meaning of new words.

4. BOOK CLUBS/LITERATURE CIRCLES *(student-led and -directed)*
   Students raise their own questions about a book to comprehend the meaning of the story. They learn to support their position by citing specific examples from the book. This encourages listening, valuing diverse interpretations of a story, and building community.

5. WRITTEN RESPONSES TO READING *(student works independently)*
   Teacher models and students practice retelling, summarizing, making personal connections to, and critically analyzing texts.

6. FREE-CHOICE READING *(student works independently)*
   Students read for meaning and solve problems on their own.

7. BOOK CONFERENCES *(teacher-led and student-led)*
   Students share with a partner or the teacher books they've read by themselves. Teachers can support readers and help them refine reading strategies. Students converse about their books and record the highlights of their discussions on a Partner Book-Conference Form.

CHAPTER 6

Finding Topics for Writing Conferences

When students step into their classrooms at the start of the school year, they arrive with past writing experiences and attitudes. Some have participated in a writing workshop; others have written in more traditional settings and know little about the writing process. Writing is so exciting for some children that they compose and illustrate stories or keep a secret diary at home. And each year, several arrive who hate to write and describe writing as "dumb, boring, and a waste of time."

Within the first two weeks of school, learn as much as possible about how students view themselves as writers. This information will provide topics for conferences and help students set reasonable goals.

I asked fourth, sixth, and eighth graders to suggest questions that would reveal their writing lives in and out of school. The sixth graders insisted that I include a question about reading. "What I read really affects what I write," explained one student. "And if I don't read, then I'll probably have some problems with writing," added another.

Model Your Process

Before you ask students to respond to the eight questions, devote three mini-lessons to modeling how you would answer them. By showing students how you do it, you'll get more thoughtful and thorough student writing. What's more, they'll learn about your writing life.

Day 1 Using a marker, write the questions on chart paper, leaving room between each for notes. Think aloud, explaining how you would respond to the questions. Jot down notes with a different-colored marker.

Day 2 Reread your notes and add new ideas.

Day 3 Using your notes, write your responses on chart paper. Hang the chart so that students have a model to follow. Tell students that they can respond to each question in a separate paragraph, or number by number.

Here are the eight questions, developed by students, that encourage thinking about and discussing the role of writing in their lives.

THE EIGHT-QUESTION WRITING SURVEY

1. What does writing mean to me?

2. Do I enjoy writing? Why or why not?

3. What genres do I use when I write?

4. What topics do I enjoy writing about?

5. Do I write at home? What do I write?

6. What do I know about the writing process?

7. Do I read at home? What kinds of books do I enjoy?

8. Do I write letters? What kind of letters? To whom?

The Eight Questions Reveal Topics

As I read surveys, I jot down students' strengths, needs, omissions, and one or two questions to raise and discuss during a ten- to fifteen-minute writing conference. I schedule these in October, when opening reading conferences have been completed. The selections from students' surveys that follow illustrate the variety of conference topics that emerge from students' responses.

- ☀ The term "writing process" rings a bell, but I can't think of what it means exactly. (Grade 4)

- ☀ I write because there are things in my head I have to put down. I want to learn how I can make what's in my head come out on paper so others see and hear what I do. (Grade 7)

- ☀ I usually draw pictures first and then make up stories that go with the pictures. (Grade 4)

- ☀ I write because the teacher tells me I have to. I never write at home. Writing makes my hand and head hurt. (Grade 5)

- ☀ I write adventure stories at home and like these because I get to choose what the story is about. I also write letters to my grandpa in Chicago. (Grade 6)

- ☀ I like to write and read science fiction and fantasy. I have to say that I usually do not have enough commitment to finish any story I start. I'd like to know how to work out a story so I know where I'm going. (Grade 8)

The following samples were taken from surveys of fourth, fifth, and eighth graders. I've included my notes. Skimpy responses or no answer at all prompt conferences that probe reasons for lack of responsiveness. (See illustrations at right and on next page.)

A fourth-grader's writing survey. ▶

Lindsay - Grade 4   2/24/97

1. I write because I enjoy thinking up the characters and the plot of the stories.
2. I write about many different things at one time. I write fictional stories, scary stories, I also am working on a series.
3. Yes, I write at home a lot. For writing

at home, I usually use my computer. I enjoy typing my stories and printing them off. I also love to draw. I draw people most of the time. I have been drawing for almost all of my life.
4. I get my ideas from reading, daydreaming, and brainstorming.

The writing prosess is:
1. get an idea (brainstorm)
2. design charachters and plot
3. write
4. edit
5. publish
6. I improve my writing by editing it, typing it, illustrating it, and adding detail to it.

- Wow! You know so much about writing because you love it and do it! Can I read some stories?

- What is your series about? Will you work on it while I'm helping during workshop?

- Can you tell me how you edit and why you add details?

My sticky note comments.

Ashley - Grade 5   Sept. 12, 1994

1) Writing is somewhat fun for me. Even though I don't like it very much.

2) No I do not like to write because I find it boring and time consuming.

3) I like to write stories but one reason I don't like to write is 'cause I always make them to long and never finish.

4) No I do not write at home ~~because~~ except for homework.

5) I know nothing about the writing process.

6) Yes I read a lot!

7) No I do not have a diary.

8) I write very few letters but I do.

• I'm so pleased that you read a lot! What are some books you've read?

• Can you explain what you mean by writing is "some what fun," but you "don't like it very much?"

• I know just how you feel about stories being too long. Let's try some poetry.

My sticky note comments.

Though Ashley is a reader, she knows nothing about writing process.

Grade 8

Byron Galbraith - Grade 8   Sept. 12, 1994

1. Writing to me is okay. I usually only write things when it is required. I have written a poem which was okay. I also have started various stories. Unfortunately I quickly lose interest because once my inspiration has left I get bored and abandon what I was doing.

2. I like to write if I can come up with a good idea to write about. Mostly, I like to write science fiction and fantasy because they interest me greatly.

3. I generally like to write science fiction and fantasy stories. Sometimes I write poems, but they're not very complex. I like short story length when writing.

4. In questions 1, 2, and 3 I wrote that I liked science fiction and fantasy. Also that I usually did not have a lot of commitment in writing finishing any story I started.

5. I think the writing process starts by thinking of what your going to write. Next you find out who is your main character and what the problem they have to overcome will be. You then write an outline and build up around it

6. I read a lot of Science fiction and fantasy but I also will read other types of stories. I like to read alot.

7. no

8. Only thank you letters that my parents make me write for birthday and Christmas presents.

• You're so right about good ideas and enthusiasm for writing.

• Do you plan stories? You might want to do this to try to imagine the beginning/middle/end. Then you might know whether you want to invest time. Also, planning eases the writing.

Byron is candid about not finishing stories and opens the door for help.

My sticky note comments.

A First-of-the-Year Writing Conference in Action: Seventh Grade

On Keith's writing survey, there are no answers for questions 3–8. For the first question, about favorite writing genres, Keith wrote, "Nothing." For the second question, about letter-writing, he answered, "Never." My goal for our first conference was to discover how these negative attitudes developed.

Keith joined me at the conference table in a quiet corner of the room. During the opening 6–7 minutes of this 12-minute conference, Keith told me about all the things he enjoys doing such as shooting baskets after school, fishing and hunting with his granddad, and drawing. "Most evenings," Keith told me, "I draw pictures of our farm and the animals we have and hunting trips."'

Robb: I'd love to see some of your drawings. Could you bring some in tomorrow?

Keith: Sure. But what's it to you? What's drawing got to do with this writing class?

Robb: [Keith, unknowingly, opened a wide door for me. I rush to my classroom library and pull several wordless picture books that I use to stimulate writing ideas.] Look at these books—they tell a story with pictures—no writing.

Keith: [Keith looks through Tuesday by David Weisner.] Can I take it home and look at it?

Robb: I think that's a great idea. Here are two others. [I give Keith We Hide, You Seek by Jose Aruego and Ariane Dewey and Zoom by Istvan Banyai. He looks through them.] Can you tell me [said in a gentle voice] why you dislike writing?

Keith: You mean why I hate writing. [I nod and wait for Keith to continue.] I have nothing to write about.

Robb: Have you ever written a piece at school?

Keith: Yeah—and there were more red marks than words.

Robb: How did that make you feel?

Keith: Lousy. All she [the teacher] cared about was spelling and periods. I stink at spelling and periods. Most times teachers tell me I have to write two lines or four lines—I do it but I don't like it.

Robb: Don't use words on your first free-choice piece of writing. Tell a story with pictures—like these [I point to the three books Keith holds.]

Keith: I'll think about it. I don't want everyone laughing at me.

Robb: Show me your artwork and we'll talk more tomorrow.

[Keith was a terrific artist who started telling stories with cartoons and pictures that every kid in the class envied. He became the class illustrator for poems and class books. By spring he had begun to write about some of his pictures.]

You can use this survey information to schedule group conferences for students with similar needs, such as those who require help with creating a writing plan; showing, not telling; or paragraphing. Grouping saves you time because you support several students during one conference.

Looking for Topics During Mini-Lessons

Topics or conferences can also be obtained from mini-lessons, as you demonstrate how a writing technique such as flashbacks or dialogue works or model punctuation and usage. By explaining to students their responsibilities during a mini-lesson, you can easily get a handle on who understands the lesson and who needs support.

STUDENTS' RESPONSIBILITIES DURING A MINI-LESSON

☀ Listen to and carefully observe the demonstration.

☀ Try to pinpoint what you understand and what confuses you.

☀ On paper, note what's confusing and jot down any questions.

☀ Raise questions during the discussions that follow the mini-lesson.

During the post-mini-lesson discussion, record students' questions and comments on chart paper. Their level of understanding or confusion will guide your course of action. You might repeat the mini-lesson or address their concerns in focus conferences or while making the rounds.

What follows are the titles of some mini-lessons, students' questions and comments, and possible conference topics.

FOURTH GRADE MINI-LESSON TITLE: PARAGRAPHING YOUR WRITING

POST-MINI-LESSON COMMENTS AND QUESTIONS:

● I still don't get why you need paragraphs.

● If it's about one topic, why can't a paragraph be two pages long?

● I just don't think in paragraphs.

POSSIBLE CONFERENCE TOPICS:

● Organizing prewriting ideas into paragraphs

● Tips for marking paragraphs on your draft

SIXTH-GRADE MINI-LESSON TITLE: CHARACTER'S INNER THOUGHTS

POST-MINI-LESSON COMMENTS AND QUESTIONS:

● Why don't you use quotation marks? How do you know it's inner thoughts?

● How do I figure out what my character is thinking?

● How do I know when to use them [inner thoughts]?

TIP BOX

Record Mini-Lessons

Think of chart paper as the blank canvas of a mini-lesson. Display charts on the walls so they are easy for students to reread. Mini-lessons recorded on charts reflect the dynamic collaboration between presenter and students and are therefore a powerful resource for everyone.

POSSIBLE CONFERENCE TOPICS:

- How to get inside a character's head
- Words that cue inner thoughts
- Deciding when to use inner thoughts

EIGHTH-GRADE MINI-LESSON TITLE:
VARYING SENTENCE BEGINNINGS

POST-MINI-LESSON COMMENTS AND
QUESTIONS:

- When I combine sentences, I end up with run-ons.
- Why look inside the sentence for a different beginning? Can't I just change the first word?

POSSIBLE CONFERENCE TOPICS:

- Strategies to repair run-ons
- Techniques for varying the openings of sentences

Post-Mini-Lesson Focus-Conference in Action: Sixth Grade

After a mini-lesson on revealing characters' inner thoughts, James requested a conference. "How can I get inside my character's head?" James asked me when we conferred at a table in a quiet corner of the classroom. His story is about two friends, Chris and Ian, who fish in a cow pond and net a huge, wide-mouth bass with a tennis racquet.

Robb: Do you have the lists of background information on Chris and Ian?

James: [Long pause, but I wait.] I didn't do that. I thought I knew a lot about them and didn't have to bother with those lists.

Robb: [Instead of reprimanding James for not completing his work, I encourage him to see the usefulness of the lists.] The lists might help you show how each boy is different. I don't quite see that now. Why don't you make a list that includes age, families, hobbies, sports, attitude toward school, dreams, and friends. This way your inner thoughts will reflect the personality of the boy and the situation.

James: Should I do that before I pick out places for inner thoughts?

Robb: I think so. Knowing what Ian is like will help you get in his head and write the inner thoughts he would have. Tell me about these boys before you write.

[James discusses Ian and Chris, then creates his background lists.]

Now bolstered with a detailed knowledge of his two characters, James successfully added inner thoughts and revised the dialogue between the boys. "To show how they think differently," he told me.

Track Progress With a Class Inventory Checklist

The Class Inventory Checklist enables me to keep abreast of where students are in their writing—whether they're collecting ideas, drafting, researching, revising—and to identify  students I need to confer with. In writing workshop, students and I negotiate the number of first drafts to be completed during four- to six-week blocks. Then students select one piece to revise and edit, and together we establish a due date for this polished piece.

Many students struggle to meet the first-draft due dates, and adjustments are frequently necessary. Students can learn to plan and budget time in order to meet deadlines as long as they receive support from the teacher. Once workshop is in full swing, you'll have some students collecting ideas; others drafting, revising, or editing; and some conferring with peers or the teacher. It's difficult to keep track of each child without a checklist (see below and next page).

When students have settled into writing workshop, I make the rounds. With the Class Inventory Checklist on my clipboard, I pause long enough to jot down notes using the abbreviations in the key. Within five minutes you are abreast of each child's progress.

As you pause near students, some might request a conference. You can place a check next to each name and return to support them once you've circulated among all students. Do this every two to three days.

By reviewing several days' worth of entries on the Class Inventory Checklist, you'll discover topics to address during a making-the-rounds or focus conference. The checklist highlights students who:

☀ are in danger of missing deadlines.

☀ keep drafting without stopping to confer.

☀ are stuck in one part of the process, such as collecting ideas.

☀ never make a writing plan.

☀ don't use class time.

☀ misplace or lose their writing folder.

☀ request help from a peer or teacher.

☀ write nothing over a long time period.

Class Inventory: Writing Workshop Abbreviations

- C: collecting
- R: researching
- F: focusing, organizing
- MP: making a plan
- D: drafting (1,2,3...)
- PC: peer conference-content or edit
- Rev.: revising
- SGC: small group conference-content or edit
- TC: teacher conference-content or edit
- DD: deadline draft
- Self-C: self-conference-content or edit

Class List	1/6	1/9	1/15	1/16	1/20	1/23	1/27	1/29
Chnoic A.	C	C	R	F/MP	D1	D1	D1	PC content
James C.	R	R	R	D1	PC content	D1	D2	
Crysta C.	F	MP	MP	PC plan	D1	D1	D1	TC content
Lee C.	C	C	F/MP	D1	D2	D2	SGC content	D3
Mary D.	D1	Rev	Rev	D2	D2	TC revisions	DD	DD
Shannon G.	DD	DD	TC edid	DD	C	C/F	MP	D1
Katie G.	Rev	Rev	SGC content	Rev	TC edit	C	C/R	R
J.C.H.	D2	D2	Rev	PC content	PC Edit	DD	DD	C
Henry G.	C	F/MP	D1	C	F/MP	D1 New	TC content items	D1 New
Dianna H.	MP	D1	D1	TC content	Rev	D2	D2	SGC content
Adam L.	Rev	D3	D3	TC Edit	DD	DD	illustrating DD	C
Amy M.	SGC content	D2	D2	PC content	Rev	Rev	TC content	D3
Andrew M.	F/MP	D1	D1	PC content	Rev	D2	D2	SGC content

Tracking where students are in the writing process helps me support them.

Class Inventory: Writing Workshop

ABBREVIATIONS

C: collecting

R: researching

F: focusing, organizing

MP: making a plan

D: drafting (1,2,3…)

PC: peer conference- content or edit

Rev.: revising

SGC: small group conference- content or edit

TC: teacher conference- content or edit

DD: deadline draft

Self-C: self-conference- content or edit

Dates

Class List								

Sample Making-the-Rounds Conference in Action: Fifth Grade

It was the third week of school. During four 45-minute writing-workshop periods, Mira had collected lists of ideas but had not started a writing plan or first draft. Here's the exchange I had with her while making the rounds.

Robb: According to my checklist, you haven't begun a plan or first draft. Am I right?

Mira: [nods her head to indicate "yes"]

Robb: Have you talked with someone?

Mira: I don't need to. I have lots of ideas.

Robb: Can you tell me why you haven't made a plan and started your first draft?

Mira: I can't write at school. I like to write alone in my room.

Robb: I understand the need for quiet. Would you like me to photocopy your lists so you can take them home?

Mira: [nods her head again]

Robb: The deadline for your plan was yesterday and the first draft is due in four days. Do you think you can complete a plan tonight?

Mira: Yes. I can write my draft on the weekend if I take my plan and notes home.

Robb: I know you can. I'll look for your plan tomorrow, then we'll set a firm due date for your first draft.

[Mira did meet her deadline. If she hadn't, I would have worked with her during lunch and then asked her to stay after school for extra help.]

Be sure to give positive feedback to students who meet deadlines and are productive; they need recognition to fuel their writing tanks. A compliment, written on a sticky note and placed on their folders, lets them know that you are aware of their commitment and cooperation.

Finding Conference Topics in Students' Writing

By reading students' writing, you can unearth a gold mine of conference topics. It's impossible and unnecessary to read all the written work every student produces—especially if you've created rich writing experiences that include journals, free-choice and teacher-directed writing, and research projects that involve writing.

Once students select a piece to revise and edit, I read their brainstorming, writing plan, and first draft after a peer editor has reviewed these. I also read any pieces that students invite me to read. Since students and I set content and mechanics criteria for every piece of writing, I focus only on what I have taught and students have practiced. I never mark any corrections on students' papers. If I do, then I'm the one improving revision and editing skills, not my students. The issue for us as teachers is to accept that young writers cannot correct everything.

As I read students' writing, I note on a class roster any content and mechanics strengths I observe and one or two areas students can work on. These notes become topics for follow-up conferences. Sometimes I ask students with common issues—such as run-on sentences, paragraphing, or rewriting leads—to confer in groups, with me, or with a peer coach. At other times, I address students' needs during a making-the-rounds or focus conference. For students who require longer conferences, try to confer in small groups.

Using a Writing Criteria List

Topics for conferences emerge when students haven't met the criteria established by the class *before* they began to write. Writing criteria consist of simple guidelines for students to follow that help them meet the requirements of each assignment. At times, you alone might set the criteria for a writing project. Sometimes they are a result of collaboration between you and your students. Once you establish that criteria, you can focus your evaluations on what's been taught. Criteria lists also provide the following benefits:

☀ KEEP STUDENTS FROM FEELING OVERWHELMED. Having criteria for an assignment dispels questions like "What am I supposed to write?" or "What does the teacher expect?" As students draft, the criteria become a resource for measuring progress and deciding what to revise.

☀ MAKE TEACHER EVALUATION AND GRADING EASIER AND LESS SUBJECTIVE. Your comments can address criteria and give meaningful feedback to students. I write on sticky notes statements such as "Your use of dialogue showed character and moved the story along" or "Reread your introduction to see if you developed your position and made a transition to the first paragraph."

☀ ENABLE STUDENTS TO FINE-TUNE THEIR WORK BEFORE YOU SEE IT. With criteria in place, students have the necessary guidelines to self-check and peer-evaluate writing *before* you read a piece. Once students understand the purpose of these criteria, and they have practiced setting content and mechanics guidelines with you, they'll know how to establish criteria for free-choice pieces.

Keeping a record of students' strengths and needs provides me topics for mini-lessons.

Some Tips on Developing Writing Criteria With Your Students

☀ Set criteria before you invite students to write a specific piece.

☀ Adjust criteria to students' developmental needs. In a fifth-grade class, 10 students might be ready to fulfill criteria requiring correctly punctuated dialogue, while 15 might work on starting a new paragraph each time the speaker changes.

☀ Review all the mini-lessons that relate to the assignment.

☀ Create a list of content criteria: try to have no more than three criteria per list for fourth and fifth graders, four for sixth and seventh, and five for eighth.

☀ Have students suggest the mechanics, usage, and organizational skills for the assignment. Limit these to three or four that you've been working on.

☀ Ask students to select a mechanics skill from "These Are the Skills I Can Do" lists in their writing folders.

☀ Post criteria on chart paper, and hang the chart in a prominent place.

☀ Have students copy the criteria on a sheet of paper, or you can make copies for them to keep in their writing folders.

Criteria for a Newspaper Story: Grade 4

CONTENT CRITERIA:
● Headline and byline
● Include who, what, when, where, why
● Snappy lead—use one of the three techniques we studied

MECHANICS CRITERIA:
● Complete sentences
● Vary the beginnings of sentences
● Commas in a series
● Pick one skill from list in your writing folder

Criteria for a Memoir: Grade 6

CONTENT CRITERIA:
● Title
● Focus on one remembered event
● Show, don't tell
● Include dialogue

MECHANICS CRITERIA:
● Paragraph your story
● Set up your dialogue correctly
● Select two mechanics and usage skills from your writing folder

Return papers while making the rounds. If students have not met the criteria, try to discover why by asking why they have omitted a particular item. Students' answers can help you decide who should intervene in a conference—you or a peer expert. I like to work on mechanics and usage with students; I find that peer experts usually tell students what to do, whereas my goal is to help students recognize and repair sentence structure and punctuation. If students are almost there with their content criteria, then peer experts will do the trick.

Using a Group-Share Conference to Find Topics

When a student volunteers to read a piece of writing aloud to the class, you and the reader can discover conference topics. Listen to the discussion between reader and audience, noting areas that can improve through a conference.

Before initiating group-share conferences, I read aloud students' pieces from a previous year. I also share the question each writer asked the class before reading his or her piece. Examples include: "Can you help me with the ending? Do you like the title? Do I describe the spaceship so you feel like you're there?" This helps children frame questions about their own writing before they share. Next, I have students reread their pieces, think about the criteria and what they've written, and then jot down questions. Students won't always have questions, especially at the start of the year when you've just begun group share. Those who seek peer assistance might ask questions such as these:

1. Does the title fit? Can you suggest a title?
2. Does the ending work?
3. Are more details needed?
4. Have I started in the best place?
5. Did the dialogue sound realistic?
6. Do you have ideas for improving the lead?
7. Is it too long? What can I cut?
8. Should this be a poem or a short descriptive paragraph?
9. Should I leave them hanging at the end or find an ending?
10. Can you help me think of some endings?

Before group share starts, I write on the chalkboard these three questions for students to think about as they listen:

1. Can you briefly summarize what the author is saying?
2. Can you tell us how the piece made you feel? What emotions did it raise?
3. What image, part, or character did you relate to? Why?

First, I note the question raised by the reader. After students respond to the first two questions on the chalkboard, I ask the reader, "Is that what you intended to say and are those the feelings you wanted readers to have?" If the reader's intentions were not clearly perceived by the listeners, then I note that. If I feel that a conference would move the child forward, I select one that I believe would be most helpful—for example, a focus conference or peer conference. As the student reads, I note strong points and share these with everyone (see illustrations on next page).

Tessa - 5th Grade

Student's Questions:

- Suggest a title
  Framed
  Caught in the Middle

- Is the end too harsh?
  most classmates thought
  Curla got away with too
  much - Would the principal
  really fail for her plan?

Observations: Good lead-
  [Mrs. Robb]
- Dialogue - realistic - asking
  for homework and response
- Situation - trying to
  cheat and blaming a class-
  mate is realistic
- Your dialogue shows
  differences in personality.
  Let's discuss the ending

4/17/1995

Shannon - Poem - 8th Grade

Student's Questions:

- Should I give it a
  title? · use 1st line
      · Transformations
      · Nature's Magic
- Should I add a
  quatrain about Autumn?
  no - you combine seasons
      in 1st stanza - it would
      be off balance

Observations: Mrs. Robb

- excellent quatrains - rhythm
  consistent
- Metaphor of music and
  dance just lovely - "Old Man
  Winter plays a song / In March
  the Melody lingers."
  Is June too early? - It's only the
      start of summer?

Students' questions and Robb's observations during group share.

Students attach these notes to their writing and bring them to our conference. When revising, students can use these notes as a resource.

Using Students' Self-Evaluations to Find Topics

Three types of student self-evaluations lend themselves to purposeful conferences:

✸ self-evaluations of how students manage their workshop time

✸ self-checks of writing-in-progress.

✸ Self-check of their progress from start-up to final draft

Managing large chunks of workshop time poses a great challenge to students. "My kids socialize more than they work," or "So many doodle and have nothing to show for thirty minutes" are typical teacher concerns. It's important to allow students time to think and mull over an idea. Equally important is helping them learn to think about a block of time and plan how to use it. The Workshop Self-evaluation Form (see page 78) is an easy way to encourage students to think about what they hope to accomplish, record what they did accomplish, and set goals for the next workshop (see next page).

Students' honest comments can open the door for a brief or long conference. Sixth-grader Adam wrote, "I planned to make a list of ideas for my piece on fishing but spent my time thinking about other things. Tomorrow I will think about my ideas and write them down."

The next day I used his comments to negotiate a commitment to complete his list. "Adam, yesterday you did a lot of thinking," I pointed out, showing him his self-evaluation form. "Today, I'd like you to meet the goal you set and work on that list of ideas."

When you use self-evaluations in a positive way, you remind students to think about and work toward meeting goals and deadlines.

Workshop Self-Evaluation

Name _Le Mas_   Date _March 3, 1997_

I plan to accomplish the following in today's workshop:
Do research for my project. White another poem

What did I accomplish?
I read sum and got a title for my poem

How can I use my work time to accomplish more?
Talk less to blayne and read more and take notes

Here are my goal(s) for next workshop class:
Finish my research
get a draft of a poem
No talking

Self-evaluation helps students set goals and concentrate.

SELF-CHECK OF WORK-IN-PROGRESS

Before your students ask you or a peer to read a first draft, invite them to self-check by testing their draft against the content criteria. This will decrease the number of conferences you have to handle and enable most students to improve their pieces on their own.

I encourage students to self-check by turning criteria statements into questions. If the criteria called for a lead that makes the reader wonder what will happen next, students ask themselves, "What does my lead make me wonder about?" This strategy helps them determine if they have included and met the content criteria. Many start revising and improving their drafts before you read them. Those students who have difficulty meeting criteria can request a peer or teacher conference.

Some Ideas to Think About

Studying students' work as they collect writing ideas, draft, revise, and meet deadlines enables you to celebrate successes and find conference topics. The checklist on the next page can help you reflect on the writing strategies you've presented and the extent to which students are able to use and understand these strategies.

Writing Process Strategy Checklist

WRITING STRATEGY	STUDENTS' WORK
Prewriting	
Collects rich details	Brainstorming
Focuses ideas	Collects rich details
	Lists
	Webs and Maps
	Clustering
	Writing Plans
Drafting	
Includes content criteria	Has details, dialogue, and so on.
Orders ideas	Sticks to one topic
Starts revising	Organizes ideas logically
	Starts making changes
Revision	
Uses revising techniques	Numbers, cuts
Raises questions	Tests criteria with questions
Confers with teacher	Rewrites parts
Confers with peers	Reads aloud to self
Rereads work	Reads in group share
	Confers with teacher, peers
	Raises questions about the piece
Meets Deadlines	
Plans time	Turns work in on time
Works on goals	Is productive during workshop time
	Asks for extensions if needed
	Follows final draft format
	Meets goals and criteria
	Uses writing to set new goals

Reading & Writing Conferences Scholastic Professional Books, 1998

CHAPTER 7

Conferences That Monitor and Improve Writing

*I*n a class of 25 to 30 students who are writing at their own developmental levels, the writing conference will be your time to individually coach, instruct, and advise in a nurturing and caring manner. The role of nurturer is just as important as that of instructor. All writers, whether student or professional, are vulnerable and easily wounded. A writer who dares to share on paper or read a piece to the class longs for and deserves positive feedback.

Your role as nurturer is to develop students' trust and respect and show them that you care about their writing and feelings. Open the conference by responding to the content of their piece, sharing why you found it enjoyable and how it made you feel. The author will hear—and implement—your suggestions for improving the piece if you first honor the story's content.

Sometimes you might have to search hard for caring comments. Many reluctant writers put only one or two sentences on paper. Respond with a comment such as "That looks like a terrific idea." Encourage students to talk about the story. Then explore their ideas by asking questions that extend the brief text. Jot down questions on a sticky note so students can refer to them as they continue drafting (see below).

Christian

· Where is the valley?
· What does it look like? What's there? Does anyone other than the eagle live there?
· Is Widow alone in the dark side of the valley?
· Why is the good eagle called Viper?

A teacher's questions help young writers think about their writing.

COMMENTS AND QUESTIONS THAT NURTURE WRITERS

* Looks like you're writing about an exciting (scary, mysterious, and so on) moment.

* I'm pleased to see you starting your piece.

* Good start. Do you want to talk to a classmate about this?

* What wonderful drawings! Tell me about them.

* I'm glad you could tell me you don't feel like writing today. There are days I don't want to write. Can I help? Would you rather read?

* The two ideas on your list let me know your story will be funny. Do you want to talk about it?

* Like you, Jill is trying to think of an idea. Would you like to chat with her and see if you can help each other find some writing ideas?

Model the Conference Process

Students can learn to confer with one another by observing you during whole-group share, one-on-one, and small-group teacher-led conferences. Take the time to debrief students, asking them to recap what worked and what they learned about responding to others' writing. Frequent debriefing conferences will enable you to assess whether students clearly understand that their feedback needs to be positive and must include specific examples from the piece.

Fostering Supportive Peer Comments

Many of the kids I teach are so eager to cut each other down that I insist they open responses with prompts that encourage positive feedback. Knowing these beforehand helps students recognize examples in a peer's writing that support the comment. Place prompts on the chalkboard or on chart paper so students can refer to them.

PROMPTS THAT ENCOURAGE POSITIVE FEEDBACK

* ❋ I like the way you described...

* ❋ You touched my feelings when you...

* ❋ I noticed how your lead...

* ❋ I enjoyed the dialogue because...

* ❋ I laughed when...

* ❋ I felt sad when...

* ❋ You created suspense by...

* ❋ When you wrote about_____, it reminded me of...

* ❋ The details helped me picture...

* ❋ Reread the part about_____. I liked it because...

* ❋ I'm not sure I understand the part when...

TIP BOX

Questions Extend Ideas

Teach students who write small amounts to confer with a partner. Partners read a sentence and on sticky notes write questions the sentence raises. A fourth grader wrote only two sentences for a human interest newspaper story: "Last night six puppies were born. They will be sold in a few weeks." Here are the questions her partner raised for the first sentence: Where were they born? What kind of dogs? Who owns them? How big? What color? Where do they stay? This is a great technique for all writers to use when there is a passage that begs for more details.

Help Kids Think About Their Writing With Editing Questions

To help motivate young writers to improve their work, ask questions. Questions serve as gentle reminders that allow authors to think about ideas before drafting, as well as decide if they want to revise or change parts of a piece.

Keep modeling positive responses and supportive questions until you sense that children are ready to offer helpful input during group share. Organize partner and group conferences only after students have demonstrated they can provide peers with positive support. Whether peer or teacher-led, students can come to these conferences with their own questions and/or choose from a list you supply.

The Prewriting Conference

"I don't know what to write about" and "I don't have enough information" are typical comments of students struggling to collect ideas. Asking questions such as those that follow in a five-minute conference helps them explore a topic *before* drafting.

PREWRITING QUESTIONS

COLLECTING IDEAS

❋ Can you tell me about your story?

❋ Can you tell me why you like this topic?

❋ Do you need to interview? Observe? Read?

❋ Would you like to talk to a classmate?

❋ Do you need to change your topic?

❋ Tell me all you know about this topic.

❋ Can you find pictures or photographs that will help?

WRITING PLANS

❋ Have you thought about the ending?

❋ Retell and jot down the main parts of your story.

❋ Where do you want to begin?

❋ What details from your list of ideas do you want to include?

❋ What do you want your piece to say?

❋ How would you like to record your plan?

❋ Do you know what this place (a story setting) looks like? Can you draw it? Make a diagram?

The Content Conference

During peer content conferences, the student writer take notes on his partner's feedback and advice. Have partners head a piece of scrap paper with "Revision Suggestions Made By (Student's Name). On this paper, the writer lists his partner's suggestions and questions, then staples the revision sheet to the top of his piece of writing. Whether conferring with a peer or the teacher, the student writer leaves the meeting with input to refer to while revising content.

CONFERENCE FORM FOR STUDENTS

Name Matt _____ Date 4/ ___

____Reading Conference   ✓Writing Conference

Topic: Story "Rando the Monkey"

: lead sets the scene well
: felt like an action packed movie

List What Was Discussed
. Title? How does it connect to the story?
. Choice of events - how can this be more believable?
. what are you trying to say?

Matt's goal is to be funny.

in first sentence

How Do You Plan To Use What You Have Learned?
• Up Front - Rando is a monkey who fitness center
. Help us see him - clothes - red hat, shirt, etc.

. Stick to health club adventures
. falls into pool.
. locked in sauna
. swing from rafters in work out room.

. Explain why presses button - he doesn't know what to do
so he presses things - light, computer, telephone
Do You Need To Schedule Another Conference? yes

List Suggested Times For Another Conference
4/16

A fifth grader's record on a conference with his teacher.

DRAFTING AND REVISING QUESTIONS

ORGANIZING & DRAFTING

❉ Reread your ideas and plan.

❉ Where do you feel comfortable starting?

❉ Would you like to talk about your piece with a peer and then write?

❉ Are you comfortable starting in the middle?

❉ Do you know the topic well enough to write about it?

❉ Who is your audience, and what do they need to know to enjoy this?

❉ What must you include to satisfy your audience?

❉ What information can you remove and save for another piece?

❉ Do you need to collect more ideas?

❉ What are you trying to say to others?

REVISING

❉ Have you included all the content criteria?

❉ Read aloud the best part. Can you make another part as good as that?

❉ What would you like to change?

❉ Do you have too few details? Too many?

❉ Is there more than one story in this piece?

❉ What parts can you remove to focus or tighten the piece?

❉ Would you like to write some alternate leads?

* Should the story begin at a different point?

* Is violence so exaggerated that the story isn't believable?

* Are there repetitions? Do they help the piece? Should you remove them?

* Have you read any books or poems on the same topic?

* Are the settings clear to your audience?

* Do you need dialogue?

* Is the dialogue realistic? Believable?

* Are the parts in a logical order?

* Does the title reflect the content?

* Is the title short and interesting and related to the topic?

* Should you show more and not tell?

* Does the ending grow out of the story?

* Do sentences all begin the same way?

* Can you add figurative language to clarify a part?

* Does the conclusion relate to the introduction?

* Does the ending make sense?

* Can you combine sentences so the piece flows?

* Are the characters like people you know?

* Are the problems real, even though the story is fantasy?

* Do the verbs create vivid images?

The Editing Conference

The errors that students make in their writing never discourage me. Errors in writing show me what children are trying to do and let me know that it's time to support them through mini-lessons and conferences. Remember that writing takes time and that the primary purpose of learning how to use written conventions is to make the content of a piece easily understood and enjoyable. Posing editing questions encourages students to improve their use of the conventions of writing—spelling, mechanics, and usage— toward the goal of improving the delivery of their content.

EDITING QUESTIONS

EDITING FOR WRITING CONVENTIONS

* Have you edited for the criteria?

* Do you have complete sentences?

* Do you need to paragraph to make the piece clearer?

* Do you need to combine paragraphs to make the piece less choppy?

* Have you checked spelling?

* If you used dialogue, is the punctuation correct?

* Have you checked for capitalization?

* Have you pinpointed and repaired run-on sentences?

* Do you have to eliminate or rewrite parts because there are too many <u>then</u>'s, <u>and</u>'s, or <u>and then</u>'s?

* Have you placed commas where needed?

* Is the writing legible so others can read it?

* Do subjects and verbs agree?

* Are you using the active voice?

As you develop students' ability to self-edit, you'll find that you will reduce to one to two the number of editing conferences you hold per piece brought to final draft. At the top of the next page are some suggestions that my students find helpful when they proofread for written conventions. Post these on a chart so you can frequently review them with students.

Editing Symbols

Symbol	Meaning	Example
∧	Insert	I am happy.
≡	Upper Case (Capitalize)	leslie lopez
/	Lower Case	Car
∼	Transpose	recieve
e	Remove, Delete	She is not here
⌗	Indent For A Paragraph	Once upon a time...
⊙	Add Period	Clean up
∧	Add Comma	The sad silent child wept.

Encourage students to use these symbols as they edit and peer edit.

TIP BOX

Tracking Use of Conventions

In their writing folders, have students keep a list of writing conventions they are using correctly. When you read a piece and see that a student has mastered a new convention, record it on a sticky note and give it to him or her when you return the piece. Students can use these running lists as an editing tool, checking future pieces for proper use of those conventions before they hand in work. For example, a fourth grader might first proofread her piece for preset criteria, such as spelling and correct paragraphs. Then she can proofread for an item from her list, such as checking for capital letters.

Despite these checkpoints, students have difficulty spotting errors in their own work. Rather than correct them the first time I see a piece, I pencil in a check mark in the margin of the line that contains the error to assist the student in locating and correcting it. This narrows the search and helps them edit errors they've missed the first time around.

1. Review the mechanics and usage criteria.

2. Check your folder for the list of additional skills.

3. Reread your piece for one writing convention at a time.

4. Mark your paper with standard editing symbols. (See illustration on previous page.) Refer to the copy of these in your writing folders.

5. If there's time, ask a peer to proofread when you're finished.

6. Set up an editing conference with the teacher if you need some additional help.

Your Role When Student Work Is Published

It's impossible for most young student writers to proofread and perfectly edit a piece that they plan to publish. When publishing a student's piece—whether that means simply displaying it on a bulletin board or including it in a magazine—the teacher (just like the editor in a publishing house) completes the corrections using editing symbols. Whenever possible, it's helpful to edit students' work with them. In an editing conference, say your corrections and have the student write them. This lets the student know that it's solely their creation and that proofreading and editing are tasks that authors have to heed.

More One-on-One Writing Conferences

The Focus Conference

Within six to eight weeks, most of my eighth graders have completed two to three first drafts, and we are ready to schedule focus conferences. These conferences enable me to build trust; establish a positive, caring tone; model how to provide feedback; and connect to every child on a personal level. In this atmosphere, I can provide the support kids need to try a new technique or strategy.

It's important for students to prepare for these conferences. One or two days before the conference, invite students to select one draft they want to revise and fine-tune. While reading students' drafts, I jot down strong points on the Conference Form (see illustrations at right), which I take from the positive comments I've recorded on a class roster (see page 107).

Throughout the year, most of the writing conferences I have with individuals or groups involve questions relating to one of the following strategies: collecting ideas; writing plans; getting started; and drafting, revising, and editing. I respond with specific examples and often model the technique I'm coaching the child on. I'll write a sample lead; provide an example of showing, not telling; or mark some paragraphs in the child's piece. Providing feedback that relates directly to a student's piece can help children who don't "get it" gain a clearer picture of how to improve their work. It's as though at your side students suddenly have the benefit of looking through a zoom lens, and they leave the conference feeling that the strategy is much easier to use than it seemed.

Record the highlights of conferences using the form on page 13. Let students keep the forms in writing folders so they can use these notes to improve their piece and to set goals (see pages 139–140).

CONFERENCE FORM FOR STUDENTS

Name _Meg – Grade 6_____ Date _3/6/96_

___Reading Conference   ✓Writing Conference

Topic: _"Locker Room Lunch"_

List What Was Discussed : _Great honesty_
Lead about dreaming of satisfying
, the "demon with glasses" hunger is top notch
is extremely funny
• You weave your anecdotes into the story
well.
• Read aloud for punctuation - also - you might
consider moving the order of events around to make
How Do You Plan To Use What You _the piece read more smoothly._ Have Learned?
• Read abud for   run-on sentences-
Repair these
• Proof read for spelling
• Think about the order of events

Do You Need To Schedule Another Conference? _Yes - to discuss_
Meg's decision about events

List Suggested Times For Another Conference
_3/13/96_

Use this form to prepare for and document conferences.

CONFERENCE FORM FOR STUDENTS

Name _Thomas – Grade 8_____ Date _5/21/96_

___Reading Conference   ✓Writing Conference

Topic: _Chocolate War Essay - thesis - Jerry should have disturbed the universe._

List What Was Discussed _• Clear thesis - you developed_
• Your thesis   it well.
takes a position-   • 2 examples in support section are
your examples support   well developed.
positive & negative.
• Can you develop your 3rd point?

How Do You Plan To Use What You Have Learned?
• Decide my position and write that way.
• Add to 3rd example
• Work on a new conclusion

Do You Need To Schedule Another Conference? _No_

List Suggested Times For Another Conference

Katie Evaluates Sarah
                    Jan. 26, 1996
① You really showed that
   Bill and Buck were
   good friends especially
   for Bill not to take
   advantage of the break up.
② Very good inner thoughts
   and realistic dialogue.

          Suggestions
① Should the story move
   back and forth from
   3RD person to 1ST ?
② Can you shorten it? ?
③ What will the title be ?

Erin evaluates Dianna
                Jan. 29, '96

① Good story Di. Great
   ending. 3 characters
   worked even tho criteria
   said 2.
② Dialogue gives background
   of characters - good -
   sounds like an older and
   younger person
          Suggestions

① Can you add inner
   thoughts? Find places
   where knowing gives more
   insight into the character.

② Can you play with
   the lead?

③ Can I help with
   spelling? Lets meet
   tomorrow - ok?

Student evaluators emphasize what works and move peers forward with suggestions.

More About Conferring With Peers

After you've modeled the conferring process, then you can invite students to confer in groups, pairs, or by themselves. Sometimes, students work on their individual issues and goals with one another. Other times, I group students around common issues such as improving leads, adding details, finding better verbs, paragraphing, and so on. I work with the weakest students while pairs or groups confer on common issues. Student authors can record peer feedback on scrap paper, sticky notes, or in the margins of the piece.

Students reflect on peer suggestions and make additional revisions before the teacher reads their pieces. As a result, students learn to use peer support and comments to improve their writing before the teacher steps in. Though the process takes more time, the payoff is that students learn how to think about and revise their writing.

Before students confer, make sure they are clear about the following things:

- the piece of writing they are bringing to the conference.

- the topic(s) they are discussing.

- the time they have to accomplish their task.

- how they will record peer feedback.

Eighth-Grade Partner Revision Conferences:

Twenty-four of my eighth graders conferred in pairs to offer each other suggestions for revising their character sketches. To prepare for the conferences, students read their partner's work twice, once silently and once aloud. Then, to confer, they use the content criteria that they developed, providing each other with examples of what worked and questions that foster revision (see page 122).

CONTENT CRITERIA FOR CHARACTER SKETCH

❋ Title

❋ Two characters

❋ One major problem to solve

❋ Realistic dialogue which reveals character and moves plot

❋ Inner thoughts

Fourth-Grade Partner Revision Conferences:

Sandy Palmer has completed reading *Birthday Surprises*, edited by Johanna Hurwitz (Morrow), to 20 fourth graders. Pairs of fourth graders then evaluate each

Title	Main C's	Problem	B- Full or Empty	Feelings you're left with	Comments
The Empty Box	Chad - R Matt - G	Chad wants the super XX 1,000 nintendo. But Matt gives him an empty box.	B- Empty E - full	I'm mad at Matt!	It was nice of Chad to forgive Matt.

Name Sandy Zurbuch   Date 4-29-97

Chart that Sandy Palmer's fourth graders use to evaluate one another's stories.

other's stories according to the same criteria that the class used to analyze each of the book's 10 short stories. Students used the headings that follow to plan their story and as criteria to peer-evaluate and confer.

CHART HEADINGS

❋ Title

❋ Main Character

❋ Problem Faced by Main Character

❋ Is the Box Full or Empty at the Beginning? At the End?

❋ Feeling Reader Is Left With

❋ Comments:

Samantha and Ashley read each other's stories, then fill in the chart. "If I can't fill in a part," Sam said, "then you need to go back and figure out how to include it." After students complete the charts, they help each other think of ways to improve their stories.

Getting Kids to Self-Evaluate Their Writing

When students confer with their teacher, one another, or themselves, they are in a situation that encourages them to reflect on their work. However, just asking them to place checks on a list of specific items will not result in students' thinking about and revising their work.

Instead, ask students to find examples in their writing that illustrate the criteria and revisions they've made. Then have them write a paragraph or generate a list that reflects their progress. To support their statements, they should cite examples from their pieces (see below, right, and page 48).

After they complete a first draft, students can self-evaluate using preestablished content criteria. Once students have completed revisions and composed a polished draft, ask them to spread out their papers. Then have them write a paragraph about their progress and process, beginning with collecting ideas (see below).

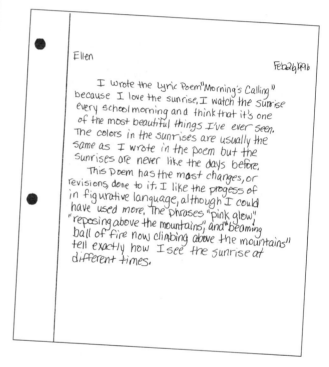

Eighth grader's self-evaluation of her collecting and revision processes.

Fifth grader uses examples from her story to support her self-evaluation.

Confer with students about their self-evaluations, applauding their progress and citing additional examples of growth. While making the rounds or in a focus conference, you can provide extra support for students who have great difficulty analyzing and writing about their progress.

Making-the-Rounds Self-Evaluation Conferences in Action

These take place as I return self-evaluations and writing to students.

Robb: You did a great job showing me how you improved your lead. I'd like you to write about the two places where you changed telling to showing. [I point to the places on Beth's paper.]

Beth: I don't know how to say it.

Robb: First, quote the telling. Then explain what you did to show and include your excellent rewrites.

* * * * * *

Robb: You wrote, "My polished draft is the best," and left me wanting to know why and to see examples.

Tommy: I can't write it.

Robb: Follow your criteria. Look at your old lead and alternate leads and the one on your final draft.

[Tommy looks and tells me how he improved.]

Now just write what you've said and you're on your way.

Tommy: How many criteria do I have to do?

Robb: All three. See me after you write about the lead and I'll help you with adding details.

Focus Conference in Action: Seventh Grade

Jerome has turned in a blank self-evaluation sheet on top of his writing. I pull up a chair and sit next to him.

Robb: Can you tell me why you didn't ask for help?

Jerome: I thought I could do it. I don't know how to start.

Robb: Let me show you how I do it. I think aloud, saying, "I know I added details. I'll look at my first draft and my final and find one place I did this."

Jerome: I can say it but I can't write it. And I added stuff everywhere.

Robb: You can write about one place and then say you did it in five other places. Let me show you how writing resembles what you're saying—but on paper.

[I write as Jerome watches and reads.]

Jerome: I think I can do that.

Robb: Think aloud how you improved the lead. Then try writing. I'll help if you get stuck. [Jerome completes this, and I ask him to think aloud and write about one place he changed telling to showing.]

Often students don't have a clear picture of what their self-evaluation should look like. Sitting side-by side and walking them through the process can help.

T I P   B O X

Examples and Self-Evaluations

In a mini-lesson, model how you would find in a piece of writing examples that relate to criteria and one or two of the conference prompts. Reread your piece and think aloud, showing students how you find examples of the criteria. On chart paper, write a paragraph or generate a list that describes your progress. You can also pass out work completed by former students. Remove students' names before sharing these with your present class.

Some Ideas to Think About

The writing conference enables you to transmit your expectations to each student—expectations that are high and that match the development of each student. Through conferences, you can discover where students are and gently move them forward by nurturing and caring for them as human beings and as young writers. Students can work independently, in pairs, or in small groups to tackle similar problems, such as showing, not telling, rewriting leads, and repairing run-on sentences.

Once students trust and respect you, they will feel safe enough to tell you their struggles and fears. Eventually they'll learn to productively confer with themselves. The statements that follow can help you reflect on expectations that encourage students to think about their writing and come up with solutions, rather than looking to you for all the answers.

CONFERENCE EXPECTATIONS FOR TEACHERS AND STUDENTS

- Give students time to think about ways they can improve their piece.

- Allow students to do most of the talking during a conference.

- Let students make corrections and revisions.

- Set goals with students and act as a guide, insuring that their goals are reasonable and attainable.

- Communicate to students that the pleasure of learning is in achieving goals through hard work.

- Make specific suggestions that can help improve students' writing .

- Don't shy away from offering input after students have discussed their work.

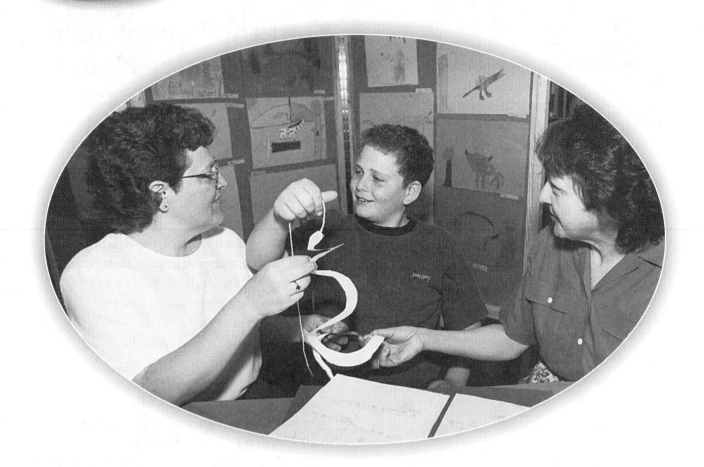

CHAPTER 8

Getting Families Involved

arents want their children to enjoy learning at school and to progress socially and academically. To fulfill parents' goals, teachers work diligently and hope that parents will get involved with their kids' learning at home, as well as support their children's teachers and curriculum. A meaningful and supportive relationship between parents and teachers develops when there is ongoing communication and when parents feel in touch and involved with their children's learning.

By having parents complete an Information Sheet (see page 16) or inviting them to conferences, you can collect valuable information about your students. The greater the home-school communication, the better parents understand changes in classroom practices and their child's strengths and needs. Here is a list of ways you can connect parents to their children's school lives:

- Letters from teacher to parent and student to parent

- Parent Information Sheet

- Telephone conferences

- Parent-teacher conference

- Parent-student conference

- Parent-teacher-student conference

- List of ways parents can help at home

- Parent education

- Teachers and Parents as Readers' Groups

- Parent-student buddy-reading

Start the School Year With a Letter Home

As soon as conferences became an integral part of my curriculum, I stopped sending students' papers home. I wanted students' work at school so they could self- and peer-evaluate, make selections for portfolios, and monitor their goals and progress. With all of their work at school, I could select items for Reading Folders and also review a series of written pieces to evaluate students' progress as writers and identify trouble spots that warranted extra support.

Keeping students' work at school is a change from the traditional pattern of sending work folders home each week or bimonthly. A letter home, like the one on the next page, explains the changes I've made. Note that I was careful to include ways I planned to communicate with parents and how they could see their child's work. Such a letter lays the foundation for parent participation throughout the year and can include information about other areas of the curriculum.

Sample Letter to Parents

August, 1997

Dear Families,

I want to welcome you and your child to my classroom, I look forward to meeting you and getting to know you. In this letter, I want to take the time to explain parts of my reading and writing program.

Attached to this letter is an Information Sheet, which I would like you to fill out and return to school, and a list of suggestions for encouraging your child to read and write at home. I value all the information you can give me about your child's interests and learning patterns. The more I know about your child, the better equipped I am to support development in reading and writing.

This year, all of your child's reading and writing papers will be kept at school. Students use their papers to point out progress, set goals, request extra help from me or a classmate, and make selections for their portfolios. I read students' papers to evaluate growth, determine the skills I must teach and reteach, and figure out ways to support every child. If students are to learn how to improve their reading and writing, then they need to study their work to discover growth over short and long periods of time, and also understand areas that require additional practice.

You will have an opportunity to see your child's work at conferences and when your child writes a letter home and attaches some papers for you to review, write about, and return to school. Anytime you wish to come to our classroom to look through your child's notebooks and folders, please do so. If your work schedule doesn't permit a school visit, then call me, and I will photocopy some of your child's work and send that home.

I thought it would be helpful to give you a list of ways you can help your child enjoy reading and writing at home. During the year, when we confer at school and on the telephone, you can ask questions about these suggestions. Throughout the year, your child and I will keep you informed about the reading and writing program in grade ___.

I look forward to working with you to help your child enjoy reading and writing and to improve your child's reading and writing skills.

Sincerely,

Ways You Can Help Your Child Read and Write at Home

When you listen to your child read or talk about books and when you read your child's writing, emphasize what you child does well. If you have concerns, please call me so that we can explore ways to support your child's progress.

* Sign up for a library card at your neighborhood library. It's free and provides your child with all kinds of books and magazines to read.

* Make weekly or bimonthly trips to the library so your child can browse through books and make selections.

* Check your library's schedule for free programs with visiting authors and special read-aloud events, such as poetry readings.

* Negotiate with your child the amount of television watched. I suggest no more than 30 minutes a day during the week and 1 hour a day on weekends. This excludes special sports events and outstanding educational programs.

* Encourage your child to tell you about a book she's reading or one her teacher is reading aloud.

* Read parts of your local newspaper with your child.

* Tell your child about the magazines or books you're reading.

* Establish times when the family listens to one person read aloud.

* Set aside bookshelf room for your child's personal home library.

* Encourage children to use part of their allowance money to buy books through a school book club or at a neighborhood bookstore.

* Invite your child to write lists before shopping for clothing, supplies, gifts, and party items.

* Have your child write thank-you notes for gifts.

* Encourage your child to write letters to friends and relatives.

* Engage in talk about movies, school, parties, sports activities, and so on. Ask questions that extend the talk. Talking is a good way to practice developing ideas and enriching vocabulary. Vocabulary knowledge improves reading comprehension. Interactive talk stimulates memory and helps young writers organize their thoughts.

Reading & Writing Conferences Scholastic Professional Books, 1998

Preparing for Parent-Teacher Conferences

Most schools formally schedule two 20-minute parent-teacher conferences into their yearly calendar. On a particular day or week in the fall and spring, parents confer with classroom teachers. During these conferences, parents receive report cards or mid-marking period grades and/or comments that evaluate children's progress.

Parents come to conferences seeking specific information about their child's progress and hoping for positive comments from teachers. "I want to know how my child is doing" and "I want the teacher to listen to my concerns and questions" are two comments parents make again and again.

To better satisfy parents' hunger for information during these conferences, I send home about a week in advance a note inviting them to reflect on and jot down issues, questions, and concerns. This has made a tremendous difference in our conferences. Parents arrive feeling involved in the process—and they therefore "bring more to the party."

- **YOUR ROLE DURING THE CONFERENCE.** Listen to parents' issues and concerns and show them examples of students' work, conference record-sheets, and teacher-observation notes in order to discuss academic and social progress. When you keep students' work at school, it's easy to dip into reading or writing folders, portfolios, journals, and Reading Logs to collect evidence for conferences. Besides students' portfolios, you might want to select several significant items. Clip these together and place the Parent-Teacher

Conference Form (see page 132) on top. Before the conference, complete the section headed "Topics the Teacher Wishes to Discuss."

This form invites you to plan and record the key points before you hold conferences.

After welcoming the parents, review the conference agenda and explain that in addition to hearing parent concerns, you want them to look over their child's work. Tell them that as they talk, you will note the issues raised on the form.

Parent-Teacher Conference Form

Child's Name _____ **Date** _____

Name of Adults Who Attended _____

_____

Teacher _____

Topics the Teacher Wishes to Discuss:

Issues, Questions, Concerns Parents' Raised:

Recommendations and Goals:

Additional Teacher Comments:

Tips for Making the Most of Parent-Teacher Conferences

* WELCOME (2 minutes): Put families at ease. Let them know how pleased you are to see them, and comment on past interactions.

* CONFERENCE OVERVIEW (2 minutes): Explain the time limits, and present an agenda based on the Parent-Teacher Conference Form.

* PARENT TALKS (7 minutes): Teacher listens carefully. Parent reviews child's work.

* TEACHER TALKS (5 minutes): Weave the parents' concerns into your presentation.

* CONFERENCE WRAP-UP (3 minutes): Together, establish recommendations and goals that can be accomplished at home and at school. Decide whether or not you need a follow-up telephone call or in-person conference. Set a date and time. On a separate sheet of paper, jot down the key points for parents. Having written reminders will help families review and reflect on important issues and the support they can provide.

* CLOSURE (1–2 minutes): Restate the key points and end with an upbeat comment such as "By working together, I know we can help Reba progress" or "I'm so pleased that you've expressed your concerns. Together we'll try to help Kyle improve."

It's important to help students invest in decisions that were made without their input. Take a few minutes in class to review the results of the parent-teacher conference, and ask the child how he feels about the recommendations and goals. Invite him to offer suggestions.

Student-Led Parent Conferences

Conferences between students and their families can be conducted at home or at school. You can organize one parent-student conference at school and one at home. It's okay if you only schedule one conference between parents and students, but make sure that students have produced enough work to confer in a meaningful way.

For such conferences to be successful and meaningful, students require preparation in leading them. In addition to organizing their portfolios and an agenda, students should also explain the conference guidelines to their parents.

Have pairs of students role-play parent and child before they lead a conference. Here are some tips that student partners can incorporate into their role-plays. Practicing both roles will build students' confidence and remove kinks from the conferring process.

PARENT'S ROLE

❋ Read the papers carefully.

❋ Respect suggested time limits.

❋ Raise questions.

❋ Make positive and helpful observations.

❋ Listen to your child's reactions and explanations.

❋ Write a note stating your reactions and a suggested goal.

STUDENT'S ROLE

❋ Prepare the contents of your portfolio.

❋ Reread your self-evaluations, goals, and reasons for selecting papers.

❋ Create a brief list of things you do well and areas you can improve, and set one to two goals you can attain. Write these on your agenda.

❋ Explain to family members what they are to do.

❋ Explain the agenda and inform families of any time limits.

❋ Listen carefully.

❋ Respond to questions and observations.

Between January and May, students and I prepare for and arrange conferences. Parents receive from me or from students a letter inviting them to review portfolios or a folder of student-selected items. Parents' replies (see illustrations at right) illustrate their enthusiam for the program.

When parents review children's work, their letters honor specific areas of growth.

Sample Teacher Letter for an At-Home Conference: Grade 8

May 22, 1997

Dear Families,

Please take the time to review and read your child's portfolio selections and the agenda stapled to the outside of the portfolio. Your child will explain the agenda as well as the progress her/his work reveals.

After you've read and listened, ask questions about the work and point out all the growth and progress your child has made. Then write your comments at the bottom of the agenda or on a separate sheet of paper.

Your child needs to bring the portfolio to school by May 28. If you cannot find the time to meet with your child, please call one of us at school and we can make other arrangements.

Sincerely,

Mrs. Benjamin and Mrs. Robb

Sample Teacher Letter for an At-School Conference: Grade 4

May 8, 1997

Dear Families,

Our class is holding parent-student conferences on May 19, 20, and 21 from 9:00 A.M. to 10:45 A.M. We hope you will set aside time to allow your child to discuss his/her portfolio with you. You will spend 20 minutes with your child.

In the space at the bottom of this letter, please write back and let us know the date and time you plan to come to our classroom and confer with your child.

Please return the completed form no later than May 13, 1997.

Sincerely,

Mrs. Benjamin and Mrs. Robb

Date:_____

Time:_____

Names of those attending conference:

_____

_____

Upper-grade students can write their own invitations to parents (see below). On the chalkboard, I note important information students should include, such as the dates, the times parents can visit, and the suggested length of the conference.

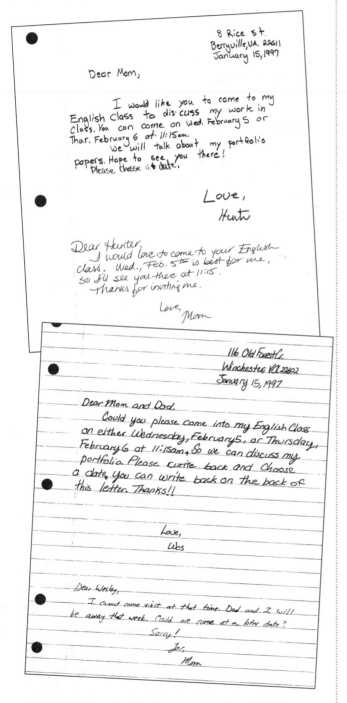

8 Rice St.
Berryville, VA. 22611
January 15, 1997

Dear Mom,

I would like you to come to my English Class to discuss my work in class. You can come on Wed. February 5 or Thur. February 6 at 11:15am.
We will talk about my portfolio papers. Hope to see you there!
Please chose a date.

Love,
Hunter

Dear Hunter,
I would love to come to your English class. Wed., Feb. 5th is best for me, so I'll see you there at 11:15.
Thanks for inviting me.

Love,
Mom

116 Old Forest Cr.
Winchester VA 22602
January 15, 1997

Dear Mom and Dad,
Could you please come into my English Class on either Wednesday, February 5, or Thursday, February 6 at 11:15am, So we can discuss my portfolio. Please write back and Choose a date, You can write back on the back of this letter. Thanks!!

Love,
Wes

Dear Wesley,
I cannot come visit at that time. Dad and I will be away that week. Could we come at a later date?
Sorry!
Love,
Mom

Eighth graders invite parents to student-led conferences.

A Time Line for Preparing Students to Lead Parent Conferences

SETTING THE STAGE

SEPTEMBER:

- Establish reading and writing workshop.

- Explain the kinds of conferences students will participate in this year.

- Set up students' writing- and reading-work folders. Students store all their work in these folders.

- Set up reading folders for students. Teachers select items for these.

PREPARING YOUR STUDENTS

OCTOBER THROUGH DECEMBER:

- Model for your students the criteria you use for selecting items for portfolios. Show them how you look at similar completed pieces to explore the progress and growth you see. On large chart paper, write sample paragraphs about a piece so students can see and understand the process.

- Students select samples for their portfolios. For each sample, students write a paragraph (or more) that explains why they chose the item and what the piece reveals about their learning.

- Help students set one to two goals that are reasonable and build on what they can do as readers and writers.

- Continue to fill work folders with reading and writing.

- Set aside time for students to select and write about portfolio pieces.

DECEMBER:

- Students or the teacher write a letter inviting parents to school to review work or asking them to review work at home. The letter explains the purposes of the conference, offers parents a choice of times to meet with their children, and invites parents to respond.

- Parents respond.

- Continue adding work to folders and making portfolio selections.

JANUARY THROUGH MAY:

- Students review their portfolios or select items from their work folders and journals.

- Invite students to reflect on their work from the start of school to the present.

- Share with students paragraphs composed by past students that discuss reading and writing progress.

- Show students how you would go about writing such a paragraph. Include a review of your work folder, journals, reading logs, and portfolio. On chart paper, write sample paragraphs so students can see how you do it.

- Students write paragraphs about their progress as readers and writers, using their work and their self, peer, and teacher evaluations to guide them.

- Help students prepare agendas for their conferences with parents. Include in the agendas that parents are to read students' work and self-evaluations, listen to the students comment on their work, raise questions, celebrate all the progress and growth they see, and fill out the form or write a letter to their child (see pages 134 and 139).

- Role-play student-led parent conferences. With a partner, students share their agenda and work and learn to respond to questions and observations a partner raises.

SET TWO-WAY CONFERENCE DATES:

- Students lead parent conferences at home or in school.

- Parents write positive comments on the bottom of the agenda sheet or in a letter to their child.

Evaluating Student-Led Conferences

DEBRIEF AT SCHOOL:

- Encourage students to discuss what worked as they conferred with parents. Students can do this by jotting down some notes prior to the debriefing.

- Record students' suggestions on a large sheet of chart paper.

- A few days later, discuss ways you might adjust and improve the process.

- Take debriefing notes (see below) and file them for next year.

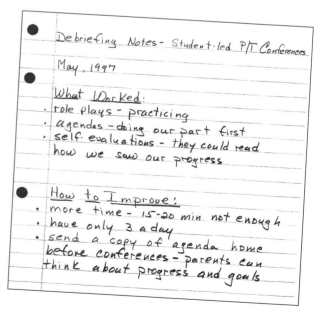

Debriefings inform you and your students.

CREATING AN AGENDA IN GRADES 4 AND 5

- Provide parents and children with a framework that you and students have created. A preplanned agenda offers the support middle-grade students need to complete successful conferences (see below left, and upper right).

SAMPLE AGENDA FOR GRADES 4 AND 5

INTRODUCTION (3 MINUTES):

- Explain purpose of conference and what parents are to do.
- Share Agenda Sheet.

Tyler Sponseller
Fourth Grade Agenda Sheet

Introduction:

Explain purpose of conference and what parents are to do.

Share agenda sheet.

A List Of What Parents Are To Do:

1. Read all of the work and self-evaluations.
2. Ask questions about the work.
3. State observations about work and goals

Student's Self-evaluation Highlights:

List of what I do well:
· Write more Neatly
· Read more at home
· Consintrate Better

List of things I want to improve:
· To final copy
· Read more

Goals: Write more at a time and read more

Parent's Written Comments:

1. Think about all the progress and growth these papers show. Write back, in this space about my portfolio and the good things you noticed.

Fourth Grade Agenda Sheet

Calvin Kerns

Introduction:

Explain purpose of conference and what parents are to do.

Share agenda sheet.

A List Of What Parents Are To Do:

1. Read all of the work and self-evaluations.
2. Ask questions about the work.
3. State observations about work and goals

Student's Self-evaluation Highlights:

List of what I do well:
Spelling better
Writing Neatly

List of things I want to improve:
learning to $
Reading Faster

Goals: learning to $

Parent's Written Comments:

1. Think about all the progress and growth these papers show. Write back, in this space about my portfolio and the good things you noticed.

What I have noticed, in particular, about your writing is that you have a wonderful imagination! The story about how the tiger got his stripes is a perfect example of this. I'm also pleased that writing isn't as much of a struggle for you, and your sentences are clearer. Your descriptions have definitely improved! And remember... the more you read the better you write!

Fourth graders' "self-evaluation Highlights" illustrate their ability to cite strengths and needs.

May 19, 1997

Tyler, I see a great deal of improvement in your writing skills from last fall to now. Do you see what you can do, when you take your time and express your ideas? Your book, How the Sahara Became was very neatly done and illustrated.

You could use improvement on your spelling. Think about the words you are spelling before you write them down.

Your portfolio was very impressive. Daddy and I are proud of you and all your hard work.

A parent's letter honors child's progress.

A List of What Parents Are to Do (10–15 Minutes):

1. Read all of the work, self-evaluations, and goals.

2. Ask questions about the work.

3. State observations about the work and goals.

Student's Self-Evaluation Highlights (Prepared Prior to Conference):

- List of what I do well:
- List of things I want to improve:
- Goals:

Parents' Written Comments (10 Minutes):

Think about all the progress and growth these papers show. Use this space to write about my portfolio and the good things you noticed. Record additional goals you would like me to think about.

CREATING AN AGENDA IN GRADES 6, 7, AND 8

With these students, I prefer to discuss the purpose of an agenda. I point out that students can invite their families to read everything in their portfolios or they can have parents focus carefully on specific papers. Students design their own agendas (see illustrations at right), and parents respond on separate paper. Included on every agenda sheet is a list of three items:

Eighth graders create their own agendas for conferences with parents. ▶

1. What student does well as a reader and writer.

2. What student can do to improve reading and writing.

3. One or two goals that student can reach during the next five to six weeks.

Student-Led Parent-Teacher-Student Conferences

Three-way conferences provide teachers with the most information about the reactions and interactions of parent and child. It becomes a shared experience in which all parties involved in a child's learning have input and can raise questions. The time line for preparing, implementing, and evaluating three-way conferences is the same as for student-led parent conferences.

Since you, the teacher, are present, you can encourage positive responses over negative ones, answer questions, and clarify statements for students and parents. You also have the advantage of hearing the exchanges between students and their families.

On his agenda sheet, an eighth grader requested that his mom look for progress and not focus on his difficulties with spelling and punctuation. "It's hard for me to do that," she confessed as she prepared to write to her son. "When I read his papers, the first things I notice are the incorrect spelling and punctuation." Sean prepared for her comments by showing his mom the progress from first draft to deadline draft. "I still have trouble thinking of what I'm trying to say in my piece and the spelling and complete sentences at the same time. Now, I can go back and edit and it's easier." The positive comments in his mom's note let Sean know that she had noticed his improvement (see illustation above right).

Seeing Sean's Portfolio helped his mom focus on progress.

Conference Scheduling Tips

I like to open the year with a teacher-led parent conference that includes the student as observer. Moreover, if suggestions are made and goals are set that affect the child at home and school, the child can also make suggestions. Sometimes parents want to discuss issues they prefer their child not hear, so the conference begins with me and the parent and the child enters at an appropriate time.

The second or third conferences are either a student-led parent conference conducted at home or at school or a student-led conference with families and teacher.

At home, families can relax and take as much time as they need. At school, if classes are in session, I schedule four to five 20-minute conferences each day when students work independently. Once families and children have conferred, parents are invited to respond in writing in an area we've set aside for that purpose. Then, students can return to their work while parents mull over what they plan to say.

Some school districts schedule conferences in the evening or reserve a half-day when students don't have classes. To confer with all families, invite four to five in at the same time, and arrange conference stations around the classroom. In 3 hours, you can schedule more than 30 conferences. As students confer with families, you can circulate among groups, clarifying issues and fielding questions.

Some Ideas to Think About

The success of student-led conferences is directly related to the preparation students receive in selecting and reflecting on pieces of work. Solid preparation takes time, and often this is difficult in an already overcrowded curriculum. The demands on your time might only allow for holding teacher-led parent conferences with the student present for all or part of the time—and that's okay.

We can only accomplish what is reasonable within the guidelines and limits of school and district requirements. However, conferences that students lead at home can enhance parent-teacher conferences and increase the communication between school and home, without eating into chunks of your daily schedule. Moreover, parents experience great pride listening to their children talk about school and learning. An important result is that parents can observe what's happening in the classroom and accept that new teaching practices can result in steady student progress.

Bibliography

Professional Books

Graves, Donald. *A Fresh Look at Writing*. Portsmouth, NH: Heinemann, 1994.

Robb, Laura. *Whole Language, Whole Learners: Creating a Literature-Centered Classroom*. New York: William Morrow, 1994.

Robb, Laura. *Reading Strategies That Work: Helping Your Students Become Better Readers*. New York: Scholastic, 1996.

Woods, Mary Lynn and Alden J. Moe. *Analytical Reading Inventory*. Englewood Cliffs, NJ: Merrill, 1995.

Children's Books Cited

Adler, David A. *Cam Jansen and the Triceratops Pops Mystery*. Illustrated by Susanna Natti. New York: Viking, 1995.

Aruego, Jose and Ariane Dewey. *We Hide, You Seek*. New York: Greenwillow, 1979.

Banyai, Istvan. *ZOOM*. New York: Viking, 1995.

Bartone, Elisa. *American Too*. Illustrated by Ted Lewin. New York: Lothrop, 1996.

Beatty, Patricia. *Eight Mules From Monterey*. New York: Beech Tree, 1982.

Bulla, Clyde Robert. *Last Look*. New York: Puffin, 1995.

Bulla, Clyde Robert. *Pirate's Promise*. New York: Harper Trophy, 1958.

Coman, Carolyn. *What Jamie Saw*. New York: Puffin, 1997.

deAngeli, Marguerite. *The Door in the Wall*. New York: Apple Paperbacks, 1949.

DePaola, Tomi. *Now One Foot, Now the Other*. New York:Putnam, 1980.

DePaola, Tomi. *Nana Upstairs & Nana Downstairs*. New York: Puffin, 1978.

DePaola, Tomi. *The Art Lesson*. New York: Putnam, 1989.

Friedman, Carl. *Nightfather*. New York: Persea Books, 1994.

Fleischman, Paul. *The Half-A-Moon Inn*. New York: Harper Trophy, 1980.

Fritz, Jean. *The Cabin Faced West*. New York: Puffin, 1987.

Gardiner, John Reynolds. *Stone Fox*. Illustrated by Marcia Sewall. New York: Trumpet Club, 1989.

Hoffman, Mary. *Boundless Grace*. Illustrated by Caroline Binch. New York: Dial, 1995.

Hurwitz, Johanna. *Class Clown*. Illustrated by Shiela Hamanaka. New York: Morrow Junior Books, 1987.

Hurwitz, Johanna. *The Law of Gravity*. New York: Beech Tree, 1978.

Hurwitz, Johanna. *Once I Was a Plum Tree*. New York: Morrow, 1980.

Hurwitz, Johanna. *The Rabbi's Girls*. Illustrated by Pamela Johnson. New York: TK, 1982.

Kehret, Peg. *Cages*. New York: Cobblehill, 1991.

Kehret, Peg. *Earthquake Terror*. New York: Cobblehill, 1996.

Kehret, Peg. *Night of Fear*. New York: Cobblehill, 1994.

Kehret, Peg. *Nightmare Mountain*. New York: Cobblehill, 1989.

Klass, David. *California Blue*. New York: Scholastic Point Paperback, 1996.

Little, Jean. *Hey World, Here I Am!* New York: Harper & Row, 1986.

Livingston, Myra Cohn. *Celebrations*. Illustrated by Leonard Everett Fisher. New York: Holiday House, 1985.

Maclachlan, Patricia. *Through Grandpa's Eyes*. Pictures by Deborah Kogan Ray. New York: Harper & Row, 1980.

Medearis, Angela Shelf, Reteller. *The Freedom Riddle*. Illustrated by John Ward. New York: Lodestar, 1995.

Paterson, Katherine. *Flip-Flop Girl*. New York: Lodestar, 1994.

Reiss, Johanna. *The Journey Back*. New York: Harper Keypoint, 1976.

Scieszka, Jon. *The Not So Jolly Roger*. Illustrated by Lane Smith, New York: Puffin, 1991.

Scieszka, Jon. *Tut, Tut*. Illustrated by Lane Smith. New York: Viking, 1997.

Schnur, Steven. *The Shadow Children*. Illustrated by Herbert Tauss. New York: Morrow, 1994.

Schwartz, Alvin. *More Scary Stories to Tell in the Dark*. Drawings by Stephen Gammell. New York: The Trumpet Club, 1990.

Van Leeuwen, Jean. *Bound for Oregon*. Pictures by James Watling. New York: Dial, 1995.

Wiesner, David. *Tuesday*. New York: Clarion Books, 1992.